D1502165

FRENCH PARTIES
AND POLITICS
1871–1921

FRENCH PARTIES AND POLITICS
1871–1921

WITH A NEW SUPPLEMENTARY
CHAPTER DEALING WITH
1922–1930

BY

ROGER H. SOLTAU, M.A.

NEW YORK
RUSSELL & RUSSELL · INC
1965

FIRST PUBLISHED IN 1930
REISSUED, 1965, BY RUSSELL & RUSSELL, INC.
L. C. CATALOG CARD NO: 65-18832

Reprinted from a copy in the collections of
The New York Public Library

PRINTED IN THE UNITED STATES OF AMERICA

CONTENTS

4 CONTENTS

INTRODUCTION

THE student who approaches the study of French politics must begin by stripping his mind of any pre-conceived notions he may possess derived from his knowledge of English institutions. Not only do terms which seem familiar bear an entirely different meaning when applied to France, but the very basis of the political system is different. He has been hitherto accustomed to think of a country being normally divided into two parties, each of which has been in turn supplied at a general election with a majority sufficiently large for it to be able to form an entirely homogeneous cabinet. That cabinet has invariably remained in power for a number of years, and has therefore been able to carry out a systematic scheme of legislation embodying its particular policy. Not only that, but while the points at issue between those two parties were numerous and important, a large number of vital questions seemed to be outside the sphere of controversy. The fundamentals of government, the essential framework of the con-stitution, of local administration, of military organization, of foreign policy, all these were unquestionably accepted by all leaders. Indeed, with such regularity did the system work that some of its critics accused the two parties of having established a regular game of turn about turn, depriving politics of any sincerity ; and if in later years first the Irish and then the Labour Party arose, they were either bound by their very principles to permanent opposition or scarcely considered as being serious competitors for actual power.

When you approach France an entirely different spectacle meets the eye—there are not two parties, but a number which observers estimate variously from four to a dozen ; only on rare occasions has one of these parties been able to form a cabinet entirely of its own members, and to obtain a majority, or indeed more than a small proportion, of the total votes of the electorate. Most cabinets have been a coalition of usually not less than three parties, and owing to the composite character of that support few cabinets have enjoyed a long tenure of office, with the inevitable result that there has been, as a rule, much less continuity of policy and very little systematic legislation. The points at issue between those parties have been innumerable, and every one of the fundamentals on which English parties are agreed have been in France an occasion of bitter fighting. In other words, while England has enjoyed the stability of a two-party system, France has experienced the uncertainty resulting from a multiplicity of groups.

The apparent advantages of the English system are so overwhelming that one is apt to forget that in modern politics it is the French system, not the English, which is the normal, America being the only other country in which a two-party system and homogeneous cabinets have prevailed. In every other democratic European State, numerous groups and government by short-lived coalition ministries have been and still are the rule ; and this complexity is not simply due to the Republican system, for it was to be found in Monarchical France (after the Restoration of 1814) and in Imperial Prussia. It is in fact inevitable in any country where the fundamentals are themselves matters of dispute, where social and economic conditions have brought political power within the reach of all social classes, and where a highly developed and widely diffused education, coupled with a strong spirit of individualism, creates keenness of political thought and numerous political and social theories. This individualism of opinion renders impossible any measure of agreement on a large number of subjects, and thus destroys the discipline which is the foundation of any party organization.

The political systems of Great Britain and France are in fact fundamentally different. They are the outcome of widely diverging political evolutions, they represent radically different political temperaments, and stand for opposite political philosophies. The Republican Constitution of present-day France was built on the ruins of a series of constitutional experiments beginning in 1789, ending in 1875. It is a deliberate creation. It does not pretend to be a harmony of conflicting ideals or to be the product of a slow evolution—it was made to solve a specific problem at a particular time, and its claims to permanence rest solely upon its practical efficiency. And underlying all those experiments, underlying the Republican Constitution itself, there remains a highly elaborate, highly centralized administrative machinery, functioning equally under King, Emperor, or President, and which, while ministers come and go, goes on working, slowly, cumbrously, but very effectively as far as its aim is to ensure the complete domination of the executive over the life of the ' administrés et contribuables ' as the free citizens of democratic France are called by their administrative and taxing autocrats. We must not be deceived by terms ; there is not necessarily more real individual liberty, or a more direct control of the government by the people and for the people in a republic than in a monarchy ; [1] and an analysis of the essence and spirit of the French system will show much which is quite irreconcilable with the principles of ' liberty, equality, and fraternity ' upon which it is supposed to rest.

[1] See on this subject Caudel's *Nos libertés politiques*, a penetrating criticism of French ideas of ' liberty '.

FRENCH PARTIES AND POLITICS

CHAPTER I

THE CONSTITUTION

§ 1. *The Republican Form of Government*

THE National Assembly summoned in January 1871 to ratify the Peace Treaty with Germany after the disastrous Franco-Prussian War found itself entrusted with the further task of framing a permanent constitution for France.

This was no easy matter. There was, indeed, no question of recalling Napoleon III after his humiliating surrender on the battlefield of Sedan, but each of the other political systems overthrown during the nineteenth century had its supporters. Would France recall the old royal line of the Bourbons, in the person of the Comte de Chambord, descendant of Charles X ? or the Comte de Paris, heir to the junior branch, the Orleans family ? As the Assembly contained a clear majority of Royalists, one of these two courses seemed the likeliest ; but which of the two ? The Royalist forces were hopelessly divided ; neither of the two pretenders would make way for the other ; and in fact, each of them thought the establishment of a republic to be a lesser evil than his rival's success.

A republic therefore it had to be, but the term covered a great variety of political systems from the virtual dictatorship of a popularly elected President to a direct democracy on the Swiss model. However, what might have given rise to endless discussions was settled by sheer necessity. The Royalists wished for a government that would be monarchical in all but name. Convinced as they were that their differences would one day be composed, their object was to set up a system that would make a royalist restoration easy ; and they turned for a model not to existing republics but to the one country that combined representative institutions with monarchy, Great Britain.   Hence the likeness between the French parliamentary republic and the British parliamentary monarchy.

To this scheme the Republicans raised no opposition. They shelved their differences, and agreed to accept any kind of republic, as long as it bore the magic name, trusting that its superior virtues would win over the majority of the Royalists before the reconciliation of the two pretenders, or the death of one of them, made a Royalist restoration possible. In a sense, therefore, the matter resolved itself into a race against time which the Republicans won : the Royalists bungled every chance they had of success between 1871 and 1877, and by the time they had composed all their dissensions they had lost their majority in the country.

The form of the new republic was finally settled by the constitutional law of 1875.   It is a brief document, strictly practical, containing no enunciation of theoretical principles, leaving many important questions undefined, and taking for granted the continuance of anything that was not formally superseded, as for instance of the whole administrative machinery bequeathed by Napoleon I to successive governments. From the point of view of the lawyer, it stands midway between strictly rigid and flexible constitutions ; revision needs a special procedure —a joint sitting of both Houses, to discuss points on which they have previously separately agreed—but the procedure is fairly simple, and there is no High Court of Justice to pronounce upon the constitutional character of any particular law. It may, indeed, safely be said that any law passed by both Chambers and duly pro-mulgated by the President of the Republic would be accepted by the people and by the ordinary courts of law, particularly as these have no power to pronounce upon the actions of officials. The English principle of the sovereignty of Parliament is implicitly accepted by the French Constitution of 1875.

§ 2. *Parliament*

Following the English model, therefore, the French
Parliament is composed of two Houses of absolutely
equal power over legislation ; it is true that finance bills
must originate in the Lower House, but the Senate can
amend as well as reject them, and also enjoys certain
judicial powers in political cases. These large powers
were defended on the ground that the Senate was also
a representative assembly, being elected by departmental
assemblies consisting of the members of the Lower House
for the constituencies within the department,[1] of the
members of the departmental council, and of delegates
from every municipal council. The senator is therefore
in a sense the nominee of local elected bodies, but as
some of his electors have not been before their constituents for several years, and as he himself is elected
for nine years, it follows that towards the end of his term
of office a senator represents the public opinion of some
dozen years ago. The Senate has therefore tended to be
always somewhat behind the times, to remain conservative
in periods of radical advance, and radical in periods of
conservative reaction. It has, however, always been
hostile to the two extremes of royalism and socialism,
particularly to the latter. It was not until 1919 that
a Socialist was elected to the Upper Chamber, and
socialistic schemes of legislation, such as the income-tax,
old-age pensions, factory laws, were held up in the Senate
for session after session, delay rather than rejection being
the Senate's favourite method of dealing with measures
it dislikes.

The constitution does not provide for the possibility
of a deadlock between the two Houses, and there is no
knowing what might happen should the Chamber of
Deputies be determined on a policy opposed by the
Senate. Such a position has never yet arisen ; minor
quarrels have been frequent, but conflicts rare, and in

[1] A ' département ' is an administrative area roughly corresponding
to a small English county ; its sub-divisions are the arrondissement,
the canton, and the commune.

such cases one Chamber—not always the Upper—has reluctantly given way. The abolition of the Second Chamber, once demanded by the Radicals, has now ceased to be a practical issue ; but schemes for ensuring greater harmony between the Senate and public opinion have often been discussed ; one proposal that meets with considerable favour from several quarters being that it should be elected by chambers of commerce, trade unions, and other professional bodies, so as to represent vocational rather than geographical constituencies. The institution of joint sittings in cases of conflict is also a likely reform of the near future.

The Chamber of Deputies is elected by all males of twenty-one years and over, no one having more than one vote, and all elections being held on the same day. Constituencies have varied since 1875 from single-member areas to large districts, such as the department, in which each elector votes for a whole list. This latter system was restored for the last elections, coupled with a cumbrous system of proportional representation, to which further reference will be made later. Whereas the Senate is never dissolved, one third being renewed every three years, the Chamber of Deputies is elected as a whole for four years. In theory, it can be dissolved by the President of the Republic with the consent of the Senate, but in practice it is never dissolved. The one attempt made in 1877, in consequence of a conflict between the President and the Chamber, resulted in a presidential defeat, and dissolution as a means of solving deadlocks or of clearing up a confused political situation has never become part of French political life. A newly elected Chamber knows therefore that its tenure is perfectly safe for the next four years. The consequences of this are obvious : it makes the French Parliament far more powerful than ours. In case of a conflict with the Cabinet, the latter cannot hold out any threat of dissolution : it has no alternative but to submit or resign—hence one of the causes for that distressing feature of French politics, the short life of a French Cabinet.

This security of tenure is not the only factor in the power of the French Chamber. It is its own master in that it not only elects its President—who only holds office for one session, is not always re-elected, and is by no means the nominee of the Cabinet—but also makes its own time-table and controls its own affairs quite independently of the Prime Minister. Its sittings are short, but its reference of all routine matters and of the preliminary stages of any measures to standing or special committees enables it to dispose of business more quickly than the British Parliament, and even to devote more time to private member legislation.

The extremely slight hold which the Cabinet has over Parliament is still further weakened by the system of ' interpellations ' or challenges, by which any member can call upon a minister to explain his policy over any particular point. These interpellations give rise to a general debate, and always end with a resolution prior to proceeding with the business of the day, or ' ordre du jour '. Should a hostile resolution be passed, the ministry resigns ; and it is significant that three ministries out of five have fallen over an adverse ' ordre du jour '. The interpellation is therefore a very powerful weapon in the hands of the opposition ; and while it helps to secure parliamentary control over ministerial policy, it has also increased the tendency to ministerial instability.

The principle underlying this close control of the ministry by Parliament is that Parliament is not merely a legislative assembly, but that its chief function is to see that the country is properly governed, and to turn out a ministry or any official that governs badly. Indeed, control of local administration is an important part of a deputy's work, and we shall see in a later chapter that he plays a great part in local affairs. This intrusion of the legislative power into the province of the executive is so constant that it has been remarked that the Cabinet only really governs when Parliament is not sitting, and it is a cause of constant friction, for which there is no remedy as long as politics and administration are as closely interwoven as they are in France.

On the whole, the legislative output of French Parliaments is small. Few Cabinets have a life long enough in which to make any far-reaching plans, and if it were not that measures proposed by one ministry are frequently taken up again by a later Cabinet, very few laws indeed would be made. Fortunately bills do not drop at the end of a session or even of a legislature, and can always be taken up again at the stage where they were left. The large powers wielded by officials and the widespread disbelief in the efficacy of legislation also tend to diminish the importance of the purely legislative work of a French Parliament.

Far from weakening Parliament, as in some countries, the war strengthened it. It sat uninterruptedly during the whole of the hostilities, and exercised a daily control through special commissions over every department of political and military life, particularly in matters of supplies and military organization outside the front zone.

The war has not brought the suffrage to Frenchwomen. A Women's Suffrage Bill recently passed the Chamber of Deputies, but was thrown out by the Senate, and it is probably not unfair to say that a good many deputies only voted for the Bill because they knew that it would not get through the other House. The fact is that whereas the introduction of women's suffrage in England does not seem so far to have seriously disturbed the balance of parties, the introduction of the women's vote in France would have consequences which are difficult to foretell. There is no doubt that the Catholic Church has in France a much greater influence over women than over men, and its political opponents are afraid that the immediate result of women's suffrage would be a considerable strengthening of the Conservative parties, and in France as in Belgium, Radicals and Socialists tend to regard the women's vote with considerable misgivings. At the present moment the question cannot be said to be in the forefront of the programme of any party.

§ 3. *The President*

The constitution is remarkably silent about the executive authority. It says nothing concerning the manner in which the Cabinet is to be chosen, save that the President is responsible for the appointment of ministers, and in fact lays down none of what may be called the essentials of Cabinet Government. The reasons for these reticences are partly ignorance as to how the scheme would work, but chiefly the desire of the Royalist majority not to fetter the King of to-morrow. Thus there is no law establishing collective responsibility and therefore the resignation of the whole Cabinet owing to the defeat of one minister ; no rule that the ministry should resign if defeated ; nothing to say whether ministers should be members of either House. In strict theory, there is apparently very little to prevent the President from selecting his Cabinet on the American system ; and both Thiers, who was ' head of the executive authority ' from 1871 to 1873, and his successor, Marshal McMahon, conceived of the post very much along those lines.

But when after 1877 there was in the Chamber of Deputies a majority hostile to the presidential policy, it became clear that an apparently innocuous clause of the constitution was going to make such an attitude impossible. Following the traditions of constitutional monarchy, and not wishing to have a president who would follow a policy really hostile to Parliament, the Assembly had decided to make the President politically irresponsible, save in cases of high treason, and ensured this irresponsibility by demanding the countersignature of some Minister of State to every Presidential decree, thus making the minister, not the President, legally responsible to Parliament and the country for every act of policy.[1]

It may be questioned whether the Assembly really wished to make the President a political cipher ; it is probable that in their opinion the ministerial counter-signature would only act as a guarantee of the strictly constitutional character of the President's action. But the ministers interpreted this differently, and insisted that being ultimately responsible for policy they must initiate it ; and that it was the President's signature, not their own, that must be regarded as a mere legal form. In addition to this, Parliament insisted from the start on its right to demand by a vote of no confidence the resignation

[1] Cf. Bompard, *Le Veto du Président de la République.*

of any ministry they disliked, whether or no it had the support of the President. It was on this point that McMahon tried to pit his will against that of Parliament by dissolving a Republican Chamber immediately after a general election ; and his sweeping defeat at the polls settled finally the vexed question : since 1877 it has never been disputed that the President can only keep in office a ministry that enjoys a majority in the chamber, that the whole ministry must resign if it is defeated on any important point, and that it is responsible for the conduct of general policy.

Within these general principles, however, it is difficult to state very accurately the exact extent of the power actually exercised by the President. As a rule, he has a certain amount of choice in the selection of a Premier ; the multiple party system of France, to which fuller reference will be made later, rarely marks out one man as the only possible successor to a fallen Premier ; and constitutionally the President is free to call to the Premiership any man whom he thinks likely to obtain a majority in the Chamber. The unanimity with which public opinion demanded a Clémenceau Cabinet in November 1917 is quite exceptional. But it is rare for a man to be able to keep office on the grounds of his being a Presidential nominee : the swift downfall of the Leygues Ministry, chosen by M. Millerand to continue his policy in November 1920, is a case in point. As a rule, a President can veto any particular person for whom he has a specially marked dislike : M. Clémenceau was never able to hold a portfolio as long as M. Loubet was President—but even this veto cannot always be exercised : M. Poincaré was obliged to admit into the Doumergue Cabinet of January 1914 M. Caillaux, whose Cabinet he had himself helped to overturn two years previously and of whom he felt a particular distrust.

Once the Cabinet is chosen, the effective powers of the President probably differ very greatly according to his personality and that of his Premier. Some presidents have always proclaimed their complete non-interference in political matters : M. Grévy gave the lead in this, and his successor, M. Carnot, followed him. M. Casimir

Périer resigned after six months' tenure on the ground
that the President was devoid of any effective instru-
ments of control. His successor, M. Félix Faure, is said
to have exercised a great deal of influence to prevent any
reopening of the Dreyfus trial between 1896 and 1898.
Presidents Loubet and Fallières kept their views in the
background, but M. Poincaré was elected in January 1913
with the avowed intention of using to the full all powers
legally possessed by the President ; how far he would
have succeeded had it not been for the war is not known,
nor indeed do we know yet very much concerning his
actual influence after 1914. M. Millerand also declared
his intention not to be a figure-head ; and it is usually
supposed that M. Briand's resignation in January 1922
was due to his resentment at the President's interference
with his policy at Cannes.[1] All that can be said for certain
is that the President has extensive constitutional powers,
on paper, and that some of these are freely used. He can
be present at and preside over meetings of the Cabinet ;
he can conclude foreign treaties, except treaties of commerce, without Parliament's sanction, and appoint to all
manner of offices, in which his personal preferences can
count for a great deal. On the other hand, he has but
once used his right to dissolve the Chamber of Deputies,
and never uses his right of referring a bill to the further
consideration of Parliament, or of addressing messages
on matters of public policy, or of actually taking the field
at the head of the French armies. On the whole, it may
be said that the President exercises, or may exercise,
considerable influence in foreign affairs, and that in home
affairs he can play an important part if there exists close
confidence between him and the Cabinet ; but that
a hostile Cabinet can reduce him to virtual impotence.

§ 4. *The Cabinet*

We can now examine the powers exercised by the
Cabinet, with or without the co-operation of the President,
and we are at once confronted with the curious paradox

[1] According to certain accounts, M. Millerand claimed the constitutional right to demand the Premier's resignation.

of French politics, the great power of the Cabinet and its helplessness.

The French Cabinet is a much stronger body than the English. In addition to the general control of policy, it has almost an independent legislative authority owing to the fact that laws often leave Parliament in a very unfinished condition, the responsible department being instructed to work out details in a way that sometimes enables it virtually to make the act a new measure. It has also complete control of the administrative system that really governs France, all local affairs being in the hands of officials acting on instructions received from the Ministry. It has consequently at its disposal a vast amount of patronage, which is used for political ends and adds to its strength. These great powers are due to the French tradition that it is desirable to give the executive a very free hand, owing to the fear of attempts being made to overthrow by forcible means the existing régime.

But there is the other side of the picture. The Cabinet is weak, because it does not control Parliament and because its tenure of office is extremely insecure. It does not control Parliament, because, as we saw, it cannot dissolve Parliament, and consequently must yield in the event of a conflict. And the same cause largely accounts for the frequency of those conflicts and the consequent insecurity of tenure. The short life of French Cabinets has been somewhat exaggerated.[1] Several Ministries have held office for over two years, and there are many cases of successive Cabinets having carried on virtually the same policy. The fact that a change of Premier rarely involves an entirely new Cabinet means that the same minister has often held the same portfolio for long periods : e.g. MM. Barthou and Briand for five years, M. Delcassé for seven (1898–1905). But it remains true that the ' expectation of life ' of a French Cabinet is short ; this is not altogether an unmixed evil : shortness of tenure is a compensation for the extent of the powers wielded by

---

[1] But it is also an exaggeration to say that ' the French Government has been the most stable in Europe, for the same group has been continually in power for the last twelve years ' (Schapiro, in the American *Political Science Review*, November 1913).

ministers ; but it makes it difficult to carry out any systematic and far-reaching policy, and is generally deplored by all parties. It has already been pointed out that the reintroduction of the Dissolution of the Lower House by the President would probably go a long way towards removing this distressing feature of French politics by stabilizing the life of Cabinets.

Many hold that this ministerial instability is only one of the evils inherent in the present system of an irresponsible President with a Parliamentary Cabinet ; and they urge that the constitution needs remodelling so as to make the President the effective head of the executive, assisted by a Cabinet of ministers who should not be members of Parliament. In other words, they demand the setting up of a system copied from that of America or of the French Republic of 1848. They claim that this is the only method by which ministerial stability can be secured. These sweeping changes are at the present moment demanded by the Conservative parties and opposed by the Radicals, who are still haunted by the fear that an all-powerful President might make himself a life-long autocrat—but constitutional revision is not at bottom a party question, for it stands to reason that a Radical President and a consequent spell of Radical policy is as likely as a long period of Conservative rule. The strongest argument that can be adduced against such a change is the fact that the general tendencies of French political life are hostile to any system by which a single individual enjoys public authority for a long while—and that the inability which French majorities have always shown to treat minorities with moderation, with the inevitable result that minorities are not apt to accept loyally the rule of the prevailing majority, would not augur well for the success of any system which gave anybody, individual or party, the free exercise of power for a guaranteed number of years.[1]

[1] For a fuller discussion of this question see our article on 'The Present Position of the French President' in *Economica*, May 1921.

CHAPTER II

§ 1. *Napoleonic Centralization*

'DEMOCRACY', says Professor Graham Wallas, 'is rarely interested in administration '—and that is perhaps why the French have not troubled to remove the glaring contrast which exists between the democracy of the central government and the autocracy of the local administration. In all its essentials the present system is the virtual creation of Napoleon I, although its two main bases, the subordination of all local authority to the central government, and a rigid uniformity sweeping away all local and provincial differences and special traditions, were legacies, the first of the old monarchical order, the second of the Revolution. Although subsequent legislation has somewhat increased the powers of helpless elected bodies thrown in by the Emperor as a sop to democratic theory, the system has not as yet been modified in any really important aspect.

The root principle is the subordination of all locally chosen officials or bodies to officials solely responsible to, and entirely dependent on, the executive in Paris, thus enabling this executive to enforce its laws and decrees by means of its own agents, and to exercise an absolute veto on any local measure of which it disapproves. This control is mainly exercised in each ' département ' by the Préfet, who co-ordinates the work of all State services within his area. He holds his post entirely at the pleasure of the Cabinet, and exercises a multitude of functions, including the supervision of the local police, the appointment and virtual dismissal of a large number of officials such as constables, postmen, road-menders, and elementary school teachers. Controlled by him is a whole army of other officials, who form as it were a departmental executive, of which the Préfet is the exceptionally strong Prime Minister, and over which local elected bodies have no power. There is not a village in France, however remote, in which the Government in Paris does not have an agent to whom it can give orders. Elected bodies, municipal and departmental, exist indeed ; but their powers are strictly limited. Most decisions of municipal councils are only valid with the Préfet's sanction, and, although the departmental council is somewhat less tied, its powers are largely illusory, for, having no officials, it must leave the carrying out of its decisions to government agents over whom it has no influence. In fact, its only real powers are twofold ; it forms part of the electoral college which chooses senators, and can discuss any matters, national or local, so that its resolutions are often valuable indications of the trend of public opinion. But the Préfet is always present at its meetings, and the council is helpless against his opposition. No wonder that it is possible for M. Hennessy to write : ' Although sovereignty resides in the people, and they elect their representative assemblies, it seems as if the shadow of a dictator still hovered over France.' [1]

Administrative functions do not, however, exhaust all the Préfet's activities : he plays a considerable part as a political agent. He is expected to keep the Government supplied with full information concerning the general condition of the department, public opinion, the effect of particular legislation ; nothing, in fact, is outside the scope of his interference. It is commonly said that a good Préfet is the one who ensures government majorities in his area : and the influence of officials in elections was one of the principal criticisms levelled against the ' stagnant ponds ' of single-member constituencies, the idea being that it is much harder to exert such an influence in large constituencies returning several members.

To the enormous powers wielded by the Préfet there is therefore but one check—his dependence on the Cabinet —and were the Cabinet able to expect a long term of office, its nominees would become permanent local despots. But the shortness of ministries has its repercussion on the administrative system. A change of Ministry does not indeed entail a wholesale dismissal of Préfets—the American spoils system has no counterpart in French politics—but there is rarely for long between

[1] *Les Régions de la France,* p. 220.

Préfet and Cabinet the intimate union of identical policies, and once a Préfet is no longer certain of being supported by Paris whatever he does, his powers are automatically checked to a very great extent. Further, the very direct control which Parliament exercises over the Cabinet gives a Deputy great power, and he is therefore able to put considerable pressure on the officials within his constituency ; for should they resist, he can threaten to demand their dismissal as a condition of his support to the Ministry, and it has been said that ' the real heir of Napoleon is not the Préfet but the Deputy '.

Administration is further complicated by the Préfet's obligation to refer to Paris for decision many matters of no great apparent importance. The direct authorization of the Minister of the Interior is needed, for instance, for the widening of streets when involving forced sales, and for the exploitation of any mineral water springs ; that of the Minister for Public Works for the making of any public inquiry as to the need for a tramway ; that of the Minister of Finance for the opening of a post office or of a tobacco shop ; that of the Minister of Education for the building of a school or for the setting up of a school library committee. As to the delays caused by such methods, it is enough to state that nineteen formalities are necessary for the fencing-in of a field which borders on a main road, twenty-four for the building of a hut on a piece of waste land. We leave it to our readers to imagine how easy it is with such a system to set about rebuilding the devastated areas of northern France.

This idea that ' government consists in holding France at the end of a telegraph wire starting from Paris ' [1] is further strengthened by the peculiar French conception that the Government must ultimately control justice as well as administration. Not only are judges civil servants, depending for promotion upon the goodwill of the Cabinet, but even they are not competent to pronounce on the validity of acts of officials. The administration must be ultimately its own judge, because it is entrusted with the welfare of the country as a whole, and ' it must

[1] Senator Waddington's phrase, quoted by P. Deschanel, *La Decentralisation*, p. 80.

be entirely free to act for the public weal without let or hindrance from the law courts '.[1]   Hence the trial of all cases in which an individual seeks redress from any official act which he claims to be ' ultra vires ' by special administrative courts, acting on a code of administrative law, dominated by the ' Conseil d'état ', a semi-judicial, semi-administrative body which is the ultimate judge of the legality of government acts.

§ 2. *Decentralization and Regionalism*

It must not be thought that the French are blind to the evident weaknesses of this system : the need for decentralization is one of the commonplaces of the day, and all parties inscribe it upon their programme,[2] but when it comes to putting forward any positive scheme, serious differences of opinion at once appear.   Some go no further than the purely administrative problem : they point out the delays caused by the congestion of business in Paris, ' a head which has swollen disproportionately through the atrophy of the limbs '.   They wish to ' decongestionize ' by increasing the powers of local officials ; they realize also that the département, useful as a unit in pre-railway days, is now too small, and suggest the regrouping of France into larger areas, such as are already adopted for military, educational, and judicial purposes.[3] But these reformers merely wish to alter the distribution of power among the agents, not to give freedom of action to representative local bodies.

[1] For a fuller discussion of administrative law see Laski, *Authority in the Modern State*, and Dicey, *Law and Custom of the Constitution*.

[2] M. Deschanel : ' We have a Republic at the top, the empire at the base. We must put the Republic everywhere ' (1910).

M. Briand : ' I am inclined to the creation of regional groups with corresponding assemblies where matters of importance could be discussed according to general principles ' (1910).

M. Poincaré : ' It is to the region that in the future all those must look who wish to lighten our budgets and to stimulate national activity ' (1912).

Quoted by Cellerier, *La Politique Fédéraliste*. See also Charles-Brun, *Le Régionalisme* ; Desthieux, *l'Évolution Régionaliste* ; Hennessy, op. cit., and our article on ' Decentralization and Regionalism ' in *Economica*, May 1922.

[3] France is divided into 89 departments for civil administration, 20 military commands, 25 appeal court and 16 university areas.

' Regionalism ' is the name given to a movement that represents an entirely different point of view. The regionalist demands not merely decentralization but the autonomy of administrative areas—the right for each ' region ' to live its own life and develop its own peculiar civilization, by entrusting to really free local assemblies, and to officials responsible to them, the carrying out of all functions which may be said to be of local rather than of national importance.

This very phrase, however, reveals the real conflict between the ' regionalist ' and the ' centralist '. The latter denies that there are any matters of local importance only. He conceives of the State not as a union of separate units, with an independent life of their own, but as one body, with one single source of authority—' France one and indivisible ' as the Jacobins called it. In such a body politic, local powers must be under the strict control of the head, just as no muscle of the body physical moves without the sanction of the brain. Before this radical difference of standpoint the details of various regionalist proposals lose their importance. Whether the region is to consist of entirely new areas, or of the grouping of existing departments, or is to be an attempt to reconstitute the old provinces of monarchical France, the exact extent of the powers to be entrusted to local bodies, and the composition of regional assemblies—all this is irrelevant until the fundamental question has been answered : is regional life a real life, demanding its self-expression in distinct institutions, or is France entirely one, with a single aim and a single outlook, and is regionalism but an attempt to regalvanize a defunct or at best moribund particularism ? It is, in fact, the old issue between the federalist and the unitary conception of the State ; but the issue has recently acquired a new significance. The reunion of Alsace and Lorraine to France raises a series of new problems. As we shall see in a later chapter, the Catholics of those provinces claim to keep a religious system which was abolished in France some years ago. This is a frank challenge to the ideal of national uniformity. In addition to this, the mere fact that the Alsatians, French as they are at heart, are Germans by speech, raises difficulties of administration : Alsace must needs have German-speaking officials, most of whom will have to be local men.   But any privilege of autonomy granted to Alsace or Lorraine is certain to be demanded by other provinces of marked particularism, such as Brittany or Provence.[1]

An even more serious question is that of trade unionism. As in England, there is an increasing tendency on the part of all trades and professions to organize into corporations for the defence of vocational interests ;   but ' freedom of association ' is held by French lawyers to be really a denial of the unitary conception of the State, and ultimately of national sovereignty.   As M. Laski says, ' When the nation replaced the crown the worship of unified indivisibility did not change but rather increased in intensity '.[2]   It was not until 1910 that the full right of any individuals to form any kind of association was granted.   Even now no association has a legal status unless it has made a formal declaration before the authorities, and its funds are even then strictly limited to its receipts from members' subscriptions ;   no gift or legacy can be received by any organization which has not been ' recognized as being of public utility '   As real liberty of action ultimately depends on financial freedom, the right of association is in practice limited by the Government's good pleasure, as in the days of the monarchy, because the Government cannot allow the setting up of associations likely to challenge any of the fundamental principles on which it rests, or of corporations so powerful as to form a serious danger to its absolute monopoly of authority.

This extreme severity towards groups stands in striking contrast to the extreme liberty of speaking and writing

[1] At a recent Senatorial election in Lorraine, which is less ' particularist ' than Alsace, the successful candidate (elected by 945 to 363) demanded ' the maintenance of local laws and institutions guaranteeing the respect of the essential traditions of the province, with the progressive introduction of other parts of French legislation after consultation with local elected bodies '.   His unsuccessful rival stood for ' the immediate reintegration of Lorraine into its full status as a French department ' (*Journal des Débats*, March 1, 1922).

[2] *Authority in the Modern State*, p. 374.   See also the chapter on Associations in George, *France in the Twentieth Century*.

accorded to individuals. In no country is the law of libel so ineffective and the freedom of the press more absolute. A Frenchman can say or write exactly what he pleases, however highly-placed be the object of his attacks, but as soon as two persons unite so as to become legally a third person, a corporation, then they become suspect, for the most innocent exterior may in the opinions of French statesmen be hiding some revolutionary agency working for the subversion of all established authority.

In these circumstances it can be easily imagined that the problem of trade unionism bristles with difficulty, particularly when trade unions were first formed among workers employed by the State, for the idea of State employees being able to revolt against the State filled the official ' unitary ' mind with dismay ; and although the law courts have so far upheld the legality of ' les syndicats de fonctionnaires ', the struggle between these and the Government is only beginning. The problem passes at this point from the sphere of administration to that of politics, and will be dealt with in a later chapter : the point to be noted here is that the problem of decentralization has brought to a head the latent conflict between two divergent theories of the State—a conflict which, hitherto mainly confined to jurists, will soon be a fundamental issue in politics.

CHAPTER III

THE FORMATION AND EVOLUTION OF PARTIES, 1877–99

§ 1. *Main Tendencies of Party Divisions*

OF parties as definite organizations based on a precise political programme there were none in France until the very end of the nineteenth century. It took a hundred years of political activity, and fifty of universal suffrage, for the conflict of ideas inseparable from politics to find what may be termed definite channels of expression ; and even now French parties are far from having attained what may be regarded as the essentials of a true party system, internal discipline and cohesion and an exact correspondence between divisions outside Parliament and the grouping of the members within.

The exact period, 1898-1906, during which parties became organized is very significant. Those years were critical in the history of the Third Republic. The ' Affaire Dreyfus ' and the subsequent conflict with the Church had thrown the country into a turmoil that approached civil war : old political allegiances and personal friend-ships were violently broken, and neutrality became virtually impossible. It behoved every one to look into his conscience and rehearse the articles of his political belief : and on all sides the need for union and organiza-tion became imperative. It follows that the principles at issue in the Dreyfus crisis are still to be found at the basis of party philosophies. Those principles went deeper than the mere problem of Church and State, although this played and still plays an important part in French political life ; the most fundamental conceptions of social and political organization were in question, and the divisions then revealed and crystallized into rival organizations are found, on analysis, to represent fairly clearly the great currents and tendencies of French political life since the establishment of universal suffrage in 1848 made national public opinion supreme.

The general election to the Parliament of 1849, when for the second time Monarchy was overthrown and a Republic set up, was, says Professor Seignobos,[1] the first which corresponds in any way to the permanent repartition of political opinions in the various parts of France. It revealed four great tendencies from which the innumerable groups and parties formed since 1849 take their origin : Monarchists, Conservative Republicans, Radical Republicans, Socialists. The definite programmes of these parties have varied greatly : measures advocated by the one have been adopted by the others : there have been times when crises have caused these four tendencies to coalesce into two, Conservation versus Revolution ; [2]

[1] In vol. vi of the *Histoire de France contemporaine*, edited by M. Lavisse.

[2] In 1913, for the election of M. Poincaré ; and in 1919, for the general elections.

and during some months of the great war, Cabinets were in office with representatives of every shade of opinion. At other times differences have appeared which made those four main divisions inadequate, and necessitated further subdivisions, but in the main these tendencies still dominate French political life, and are indeed, under various names, to be found in all countries enjoying representative institutions.

When the elections of 1877 gave the Republicans a majority and it became clear that the day of a monarchical restoration was gone, it became necessary to reopen the question which had been deliberately set aside as long as the Republic itself was in jeopardy—what definite form, political, social, and economic, was it to take? With the raising of this issue, the serious differences existing in the Republican ranks became apparent : as Gambetta said, the era of dangers was over, that of difficulties had begun.

Those difficulties can only be understood by some reference to the previous history of French Republicanism.

We have already said that as far back as 1848 the Republicans were not agreed as to their constructive programme ; in fact the failure of the Republican experiment of 1848–51 was largely due to divisions on fundamental policy : at the elections of 1869 the manifesto issued at Belleville by Gambetta,[1] the leader of the ' advanced ' group, had been repudiated by the moderates, and only the knowledge that disunion would bring about a Royalist restoration enabled all Republicans to co-operate in the establishment of the Republic. The removal of the common danger made further coalition unnecessary and therefore impossible.

The political questions on which permanent divisions appeared were mainly fiscal and religious. There were others : foreign affairs, administrative reforms; but on none of these did clear-cut party divisions appear. The war of 1870–1 removed for some years from the Radical

[1] Gambetta demanded, in addition to reforms agreed to by all Republicans, ' complete freedom of association, the separation of Church and State, a non-religious, free, compulsory elementary education, the election of all public officials, and the suppression of permanent armies as the chief cause of hatred among peoples '

programme the pacificism of 1848 and 1869 ; Gambetta himself became the advocate of a spirited foreign policy and of colonial expansion, and only the Dreyfus affair brought military questions back into party politics. As to administration, the Radical demand for the election of officials remained for many years on the party's programme, but no attempt has so far been made to realize it, while administrative decentralization is now (as we have seen) demanded by all parties.

As regards fiscal questions, Radicals placed in the forefront of their programme the substitution of a progressive income-tax for the existing system of indirect taxation and of duties on articles of current use. They also advocated the buying out by the State of monopolies, in particular that of the great railway companies. But these measures were invariably defeated for the next twenty-five years, and need only be mentioned owing to the cleavages they made in Republican ranks, for in their opposition to this policy Republican moderates were supported by the anti-Republican groups.

The religious problem, however, dominated the politics of the next half-century and must be described in some detail if modern France is to be understood.

§ 2. *Church and State in the Nineteenth Century*

Until the French Revolution, the Roman Catholic Church was the one Church that was established, or indeed legally recognized : she possessed great wealth, most of which was in the hands of the conventual clergy, and although her supreme head was, of course, not the King but the Pope, she lived in close connexion with the monarchy and consequently suffered heavily in the revolutionary storm. Not only was a great part of her wealth confiscated, but an attempt was made to revolutionize her organization by turning priests and bishops into elected officials, thus practically placing the Church outside papal control. Later on, Catholic worship became entirely prohibited and a period of religious persecution set in : the inevitable result of which was to antagonize the mass of faithful Catholics towards revolutionary and Republican principles.[1]

On his accession to power Napoleon saw that religious peace was the country's chief need, and he immediately entered with the Papacy into negotiations of which the Concordat of 1802 (supplemented in 1811) was the outcome. By this treaty Catholic worship was allowed to be freely exercised under such restrictions as were necessary for public order. The Government nominated to vacant bishoprics, the Pope instituted and ordained. Presentation to livings was in the hands of bishops, the Government retaining the right of vetoing any appointment, and guaranteeing the salaries of all secular clergy as a return for the property confiscated by the revolutionary government. There was to be a French ambassador at Rome, a papal nuncio in Paris. No papal mandate could be issued, or synod held, without the State's sanction. In a word, the Church became in France a department of the Civil Service, subject to a certain degree of papal supervision, the limits of which were left to a large extent undefined. At every subsequent change of political régime the Concordat was renewed by the new Government.

But this settlement, if it had placed on a satisfactory basis the relations between the Church and the State, had done nothing to reconcile the Church and the Republican party. On the contrary, the breach between the two gradually widened. The control of virtually all education by the clergy, the attempt to enforce in universities and schools a certain orthodoxy of political and religious opinion, the overthrowing of the revolutionary Roman Republic by French bishops in 1849, and the condemnation by Pope Pius IX in the ' Syllabus ' of 1864 of the principles of democracy and of religious toleration, all tended to make Republicanism extremely hostile to the Church ; and it may be said that even

---

[1] This question is admirably dealt with in Belloc's *French Revolution*. Mr. Belloc, writing as a Catholic in sympathy with the political and social principles of the Revolution, gives a particularly illuminating and dispassionate survey of this distressing period. See also Lilly's *New France*.

before 1870 the Radical wing of the Republican party
was virtually committed to the main principles of what
was going to be the ' anti-clerical ' programme.

The double allegiance of Republican Catholics, to their
political and to their religious faith, was thus strained
from the very start, while the political convictions of
Catholic Monarchists were strengthened by the belief
that opposition to Republican principles was a religious
duty. As to non-Catholic Republicans, they had eagerly
picked up the gauntlet thrown down, and announced that
once in power they would fight the political power of
the Church, as expressed in the Concordat, and in the
schools organized by the religious orders.

The actual overthrow of the Empire did not lead,
however, to immediate complications. The Catholics had
a majority in the National Assembly of 1871 and could
with skill have kept government in their hands for many
years, until the monarchy was restored. Their evident
interest was to be moderate, to alienate none of those
people who had no violent liking for a Republic as such
and only wanted a sane liberally-minded government of
national conciliation and reconstruction. But on the
contrary, they went out of their way to irritate moderate
opinion and to make people fear that a monarchical
restoration would mean the re-establishment of Catholic
supremacy and the end of religious liberty. Vexatious
measures were passed prohibiting non-religious funerals :
Parliament voted the erection at the public expense of
a national Roman Catholic church in Paris, and it was
actually suggested that, while German troops were still
on French territory, French troops should be sent to
assist the Papacy in the reconquest of Rome from the
King of Italy.

This policy of militant Catholicism played a great part
in the change of public opinion which transformed the
Monarchical Assembly of 1871 into the Republican
Parliament of 1877. But this change had as its inevit-
able consequence the opening of a conflict between the
Republic and the Papacy.

The first quarrel came in March 1877 over a petition
from all bishops to the Government ' to do all they could

to secure the respect of the independence of the Holy
Father and his government'. It was a scarcely-veiled
appeal for the restoration of the papal temporal power,
and was deeply resented by the Italian Government.
As it happened, the French Government was just then
engaged in negotiating a commercial treaty with Italy :
it consequently forbade the circulation of the episcopal
appeal. This led to a violent press and pamphlet campaign and to a discussion in the Chamber, during which
Gambetta made the famous speech accusing the Church
of ' turning religion into politics and of trying to impose
upon the country a priestly domination which it de-
tested '. He ended with the words : ' Clericalism, there
is the enemy.' The debate ended in the carrying by 304
to 113 votes of a resolution ' calling upon the Government
to use its legal powers for the repression of the anti-
patriotic agitation of the ultramontane parties, whose
increasing activities might become a danger to the
internal and external security of the State '. It was
a declaration of war from the mass of the Republicans
against political Catholicism.

A battle-field was not far to seek. The Concordat of
1802 had legalized the position of the secular clergy only :
all regular clergy, orders, convents, came under the
heading of ' associations ' and were under the common
law relating to associations of every kind. Now these
were always suspect to the strongly unitary tendencies
of the Government : no association could exist without
a formal authorization, and Napoleon had no intention
of tolerating in France the existence of numerous bodies
living under their own rules. Consequently authorizations
were only given by him to a few missionary and philan-
thropic orders. The law against unauthorized congregations became, however, a dead letter under the monarchy,
and many orders returned to France from the exile into
which they had been sent either by previous kings or by
the Revolution. Many of them were engaged in teaching,
and opened elementary and secondary schools, and these
became legally recognized by the education law of 1850,
although the teaching orders themselves were still, strictly
speaking, on sufferance only.

The Republicans soon realized that all they needed to weaken the Church in one of its strongholds, the schools, was to apply strictly the existing law : and the Government instructed in March 1880 all non-authorized congregations to apply for an authorization within three months. This they refused to do, and after much passive resistance the decrees were obeyed, as regards men's orders : some 300 communities were dissolved, the Carthusians and Trappists being alone undisturbed. The Government did not feel as yet able to face the problem of Church schools ; but it removed their virtual monopoly of elementary education by deciding to create in every commune a free state school and to make elementary education compulsory, postponing the dissolution of Church schools to the time when the State schools would be sufficiently powerful to cope with the education of all the children of the country.

It is now possible to gauge the importance of the religious question in French internal politics, and its share in determining party divisions. It is evident that virtually all Republicans were united in deploring and resisting any open attacks made by the Catholic parties against the Republican system. Where they differed was in the general attitude to be adopted. In the opinion of the Moderates, enough had now been done : further quarrels with the Church would only injure the prestige of the new Republic and might arouse a dangerous opposition, whereas the extreme Radicals, urging that offensive is the best defensive, wished to carry out the full anti-clerical programme of disestablishment, abolition of all Church schools, expulsion of all religious orders, and the breaking-off of diplomatic relations with the Vatican.

Had this been the only issue, France might have entered upon a period of two-party government. The Monarchists were helpless ; the handful of Socialist deputies, representing three different Socialist parties, were too few in number to offer any opposition dangerous enough to need placating or an assistance worth obtaining at the cost of any political concessions.

Personal jealousies, disagreement on matters of secondary importance, and the fact that the Republic seemed safe from attack, soon broke up Moderates and Radicals into a number of sections, helpless for action and dangerous in opposition. Cabinets could only be formed by the temporary union of several groups : there was no majority possible for a constructive policy : ' The situation created by the elections does not allow great ambitions ', said Goblet when forming a Cabinet in December 1885, and the phrase sums up the whole period.

The impossibility of governing save by Coalition Cabinets imposed upon ministers a choice between two systems : either to obtain Radical support by adopting some items in the Radical programme or by showing sympathy towards Socialism—this was called relying on ministries of Republican concentration—or to depend upon the votes of the Conservatives by maintaining a policy of ' conciliation ', i. e. refraining from any attacks on the clergy. But under neither scheme could any vigorous policy be carried out, as no Cabinet could go very far along the Radical road without losing some of its moderate Republican followers ; and as years went on politics became more and more stagnant.

§ 3. ' Boulangisme ' and ' L'Affaire Dreyfus '

Just before the revolution of 1848, one of the King's ministers had said that nothing was really the matter with France, but that she was bored. It was the same in 1889 when the Republic had suddenly to face its first serious internal danger, the Boulanger agitation. It would take us too far afield to attempt a full sketch of this famous episode. Originally a Radical, and Minister of War in two successive Cabinets, General Boulanger attained notoriety both by the violence of his democratic utterances and by his aggressive attitude towards Germany ; and thus became for different reasons popular with both the extreme Right and the extreme Left. On losing office in June 1887 he endeavoured to form a new party, the aim of which was a remodelling of the constitution on the lines of that of 1848—a single chamber and a non-Parliamentary executive. He obtained the support of the mass of the Conservatives, particularly of the Orleanists with their leader the Comte de Paris, who saw in such a system the easiest way to re-establish monarchy, of many Radicals who were weary of the helplessness of Coalition Cabinets, and of all those who were eager for a spirited foreign policy. A little weakness on the part of the Government, a little more ' dash ' on the part of Boulanger, and he might have been successful in overthrowing by force the Paris Government and in making an effective appeal to the country. But he let the opportunity slip and found himself arraigned for high treason before the Senate. He escaped before the trial, and Boulangism collapsed, leaving behind the supporters of a non-Parliamentary executive to re-form themselves a few years later, together with the Orleanists, as the Nationalist Party.[1] The general elections of 1889 only returned 38 revisionists, mainly elected at the expense of the Radicals, the other parties being left unchanged ; and Coalition Cabinets went on being formed on the precarious co-operation of the various groups of Republican Moderates. Thus did politics drag through the early nineties, a period marked only by two movements of any importance, the attempt made by Pope Leo XIII to bridge the chasm between the Church and the Republic, and the rise of the Socialists.

The failure of Boulangism had been a great blow to those who still hoped for a restoration of the monarchy : to many Catholic leaders the present condition could be interpreted as Catholics dissipating their energies in a sterile opposition to a victorious power, an attitude which, to quote Mr. J. E. C. Bodley,[2] meant ' the utilization of the altar as the substructure of a rickety throne which if ever set up would probably come crashing down, bringing with it part of the ecclesiastical fabric '. The Pope thought the time had come for what may

[1] ' Boulangism is a stage in the series of efforts made to recover her true direction by a nation perverted by foreign intrigues ' (Barrès, *Scènes et Doctrines du Nationalisme*). For a study of this period from a Boulangist standpoint see Barrès, *Le roman de l'énergie nationale*, 3 vols.
[2] *France*, p. 586.

almost be described as a fresh Concordat—the establishment of co-operation between Catholics and those Republicans who did not wish to pursue an anti-clerical policy as long as the Church was not wedded to reaction. He therefore let it be known (February 1892) that the Church was ' not repugnant to any particular form of government ', and that a distinction must be made between authority as such, which must be obeyed, and particular laws which might be wrong and might have to be opposed.

This bold policy failed. A certain number of Catholics eagerly seized this opportunity of accepting the Republic, and formed themselves into a new Catholic Republican party, but the greater number refused to follow the Pope's lead and said that no reconciliation was possible with the parties who had passed the criminal laws against Church schools and religious orders. Nor did the Republicans welcome the new allies—the Church had too long made common cause with political conservatism for her conversion to democracy to be accepted as genuine without further proof. Thus the policy of ' Ralliement ' did little, and the general elections of 1893 only returned 93 conservatives—33 ' ralliés ' and 60 ' Die-hards ' if we may borrow this expressive term. The three Socialist groups obtained 48 seats, and now appeared as a force to be reckoned with.

Discredited and broken after the failure of the ' commune ' in 1871, the French Socialist party was re-organized by the Congress of Trade Unions held in 1879, but its unity was soon wrecked by a breach between thorough-going Marxists led by Jules Guesde and the more moderate ' Reformists ' (1882). A few years later the Reformists themselves split into two organizations, Brousse holding to the less advanced position, while Allemane formed a revolutionary party to advocate a general strike (1891). In spite of their divisions, they made rapid headway ; and although they did not return many members to Parliament they obtained a good many seats on municipal councils. They lacked, however, a definite political programme.

The founder of a real Parliamentary Socialist party was a young university lecturer, Jean Jaurès, who was elected

to Parliament at a by-election in 1892 and suggested that
Socialists should ' annex to the economic programme of
the Socialists the political programme of the Radicals '
(February 1893). The result of this was the return at the
next general elections not only of a number of ' working-
class ' Socialists of various tendencies but of several
' bourgeois ' independent Socialists who included Jaurès,
Millerand, and Viviani, and whose policy was one of
co-operation between advanced Radicals and moderate
Socialists. This co-operation was made all the easier by
the Radical opposition to the laws passed in 1894 against
anarchist propaganda, and by the frank hostility of the
Moderates, or ' Progressives ' as they now called themselves, who, having obtained a clear majority in the 1893
elections, were no longer dependent on Radical votes,
and, in spite of frequent Cabinet changes, followed a
fairly consecutive policy of anti-Radicalism and anti-
Socialism, in co-operation with a portion of anti-Republican Conservatives. At no time since 1877 had Republicanism been at a lower ebb, but just as the years of
stagnation 1885-7 had been followed by the Boulanger
crisis, so the stagnant years 1893-8 were followed by
a crisis that rent France in twain, the ' Affaire Dreyfus '.

The bare facts are fairly simple. In December 1894,
a Jewish officer, Captain Dreyfus, was tried by court
martial on a charge of having sold certain documents to
an unspecified foreign power, the main evidence being
a list of such documents alleged to be in his handwriting.
He was condemned to penal servitude for life and removed
to a lonely island in New Caledonia. The trial made little
stir at the time, as Dreyfus's guilt seemed clearly proved.
His relatives, however, convinced of his innocence, began
a systematic search for new evidence. The story would
be too long to tell here. A sheer accident—the discovery
of a torn letter in a waste-paper basket at the German
embassy—showed that one of the chief agents in the
prosecution of Dreyfus, Major Esterhazy, was himself in
the pay of a foreign power, and a fresh examination of the
original list of documents (the ' bordereau ') showed this
to have been in Esterhazy's handwriting. It further
came to light that Dreyfus's condemnation had only been

obtained by the communication to the court of documents that were not seen by the counsel for the defence : and here again the word ' forgery ' was freely used. Thus, by 1898, many people of different opinions became suspicious that Dreyfus had been the victim of a plot, and began to agitate for a revision of the trial.

It is at this point that the affair enters politics. The moment the word revision was mentioned, the Conservatives declared that to doubt the guilt of Dreyfus was to attack the honour of the army and to be guilty of un-patriotic behaviour : that not only was the guilt of Dreyfus certain but that his treason and the revisionist movement were part of a huge German campaign in France acting through Jews, Protestants, and Freemasons, united in a ' Syndicate of treason ' to hand France over to her enemies.[1]

The magnitude of the issues involved was soon evident. If the ' Anti-Dreyfusards ', as they were called, were right, then France was indeed in a parlous condition, and nothing but a clean sweep could save her. But if they were wrong ? If Dreyfus was innocent, then he had been condemned by people who knew him to be innocent, or at any rate by people who accepted as evidence documents of more than doubtful authenticity, who virtually refused to hear the evidence for the defence, and who lent themselves to a travesty of military justice. It meant, therefore, that a whole number of important people, mainly staff-officers and members of the War Office, had deliberately condemned an innocent man to a living death. It was therefore perfectly clear that something bigger was at stake than the mere desire to discredit a particular officer. But what was behind it all ? At whom was the blow really aimed ? That was the question that was harassing every open-minded Frenchman during the years 1896–9. He hoped that Dreyfus was guilty and his advocates wrong, for if it were otherwise, then a vista of events opened with consequences too appalling to con-

---

[1] ' Just for having said that the handwriting of the " bordereau " and that of Esterhazy were the same, we were called traitors, and a mad public opinion suspended all our liberties ' (Halévy, *Apologie pour notre passé*).

template.   For the matter was but too clear.   Dreyfus
was a Jew and a Republican, while the War Office was
still almost entirely in the hands of the reactionary and
Catholic elements.   The more doubt was shed on the
justice of Dreyfus's condemnation, the more the Conservative press sought to identify his cause with that of
Radicalism, Freemasonry, Jewry, and every influence
hostile to the Church and to Conservatism.

It is no wonder that for a long while France refused to
face the issue that the ' Affaire ' was really a plot for the
overthrow of the Republic.   Many Frenchmen said the
story simply could not be true and would go no further.
They did not wish to hear any evidence, they did not
want the thing to be true, therefore it was false.   Others
frankly took up the attitude that the guilt or innocence
of Dreyfus had become a secondary issue ; to expose such
a scandal would ruin the prestige of France abroad, the
honour of her Army, the honour of her Church.   Therefore,
the agitation must be crushed.   Better an innocent should
suffer than risk the possibility of civil war.[1]

For civil war it nearly was, and we are glad to see that
Lord Bryce [2] confirms a view we have long held, that
France was in even greater danger than seemed at the
time.   The more evidence appeared, the more light was
thrown on the way in which the whole trial had been
manufactured, the more bitter the controversy grew.
The violence of party politics reached an unbelievable
pitch : lifelong friendships were severed, officials dismissed, every possible measure of intimidation used.

The crux of the matter was the attitude of the Government.   To take definite sides would be to precipitate
a conflict—to open the door to appalling possibilities.
So the Cabinet, not daring to pronounce for an immediate
retrial, waited.   Many among the Progressives believed
in the need for a new trial, but hesitated, fearing possible
consequences.   ' They   shrank ', says   Halévy,   ' from

[1] ' The benefit of the doubt should go to the real accused, to the
author of a doubtful condemnation, that is, to society itself.   The
right thing to do was to respect a judgement given by French Society.'
Charles Maurras, quoted by Halévy, op. cit.
[2] In *Modern Democracies*, vol. i, p. 243.

strengthening the Revolutionary parties by the revealing of the vile conduct of which certain army leaders had been guilty.' They knew that the reopening of the matter would undoubtedly discredit Army and Church, and open the flood-gates of a Radical reaction that would probably sweep away the Moderates. Instead of boldly proclaiming the need for a retrial and saving the honour of their party, they trusted that the scandal could still be hushed.

This remained a possibility until a new document, purporting to be a final proof of guilt, was suddenly found to be a forgery, the work of a Colonel Henry who, on being arrested, committed suicide. This event finally turned the scales, both in public opinion and in Parliament, and in October 1898 the High Court of Appeal ordered a retrial. The revision cause was further strengthened three months later by the election of M. Loubet to the Presidency in succession to M. Faure, an anti-revisionist ; and the ignominious collapse on the day of the election of an attempt made by the extreme nationalists to establish in Paris a temporary military government gave an almost farcical ending to a movement that had been a serious danger to the Republic. Shortly after, the Cabinet resigned and a revisionist ministry took office under Waldeck-Rousseau.[1]

CHAPTER IV

THE RADICAL PARTY IN POWER, 1899–1914

§ 1. *Anti-clerical Legislation*

THE new Premier was himself an ex-Moderate who had become convinced of the need for a retrial, but his colleagues were mostly Radicals, and the Cabinet even included a Socialist, M. Millerand. Although the Socialists had been in the forefront of the revision struggle, the question of co-operation with a bourgeois Cabinet caused acute discussion, the upshot of which was the reorganiza-

[1] See for this period Anatole France, *l'Ile des Pingouins* and *Histoire contemporaine* (strongly pro-Dreyfus). For the anti-Dreyfus standpoint, see Barrès, op. cit., Dutrait-Crozon, *Précis de l'Affaire Dreyfus*, and the works of Charles Maurras.

tion of the Socialists into two parties, the French Socialist party under Jaurès for co-operation with the Radicals in their anti-clerical policy, and the Socialist party of France under Guesde.

With the advent of this Cabinet to power, French politics enter upon a new phase. The Republican system had been in serious danger from the continued attacks of Church and Army, and the Moderates had been blind to the danger, or failed to avert it. The inevitable change of policy was, therefore, bound to be a return to the old Radical anti-militarist and anti-clerical programme, and the Progressives found themselves obliged to choose between this and a virtually anti-Republican reaction ; the party split and went into the wilderness of opposition for a long spell of years.

The new Cabinet immediately opened its campaign of war against the Right ; it placed on half pay a number of generals and other officers of high rank for having mixed themselves in politics, and pardoned Dreyfus when a second court martial declared him guilty ' with ex-tenuating circumstances '.[1] Then it faced the problem of the Church. Its first move was indeed not aimed at the Church itself, and theoretically did not involve any new policy ; it simply consisted in the enforcement of existing laws against religious orders. Many of these had remained without the official recognition which alone could give them legal standing according to the associa-tions law of 1881, trusting that no government would dare stir up such a hornet's nest as to interfere with them. But in 1900 a committee of inquiry, appointed by the Cabinet, declared that all over the country were illegal convents, possessing over a milliard francs of wealth, with huge estates that never paid duty : that the laws

[1] The conviction of Dreyfus was finally quashed in 1905 and he was reinstated in the Army. As a colonel he held a home command during the war.

' The Dreyfus affair was utilized by the Reactionaries against the Republic, by the Clericals against the non-Catholics, by the military party against the Parliamentarians, and by the revolutionary Socialists against the army. It was also conspicuously used by rival Republican politicians against each other, and the chaos of political groups was further confused by it.' Bodley, art. ' France,' in *Encyclopaedia Britannica.*

forbidding bequests to unauthorized corporations were constantly evaded by fictitious sales or legacies to a third person, with secret orders to hand it over to such associations, and that while some of these associations performed useful duties of charity and poor relief, others were merely employers of sweated labour or agencies for the propagation of reactionary literature : while the teaching orders were steadily undermining democratic and republican ideas among the young.

The result of the inquiry was the ' Association Laws of 1901 ', which declared that any association involving a common life and the taking of vows must be authorized by the State : and failing the securing of such an authorization would be dissolved and none of its members allowed to take up teaching privately. M. Combes, who succeeded Waldeck-Rousseau as President in 1902, carried out the law with even more rigour than had been originally intended : practically all requests for authorization were refused, all the teaching orders were dissolved, and with very few exceptions the country was cleared of all religious associations. Here and there some local resistance was offered, but on the whole these sweeping measures met with remarkably little opposition, and the general election of 1902 gave the ' Bloc ' a handsome majority. That the law was harsh, far too extreme and deliberately strained by the executive beyond the intentions of the legislature, can scarcely be denied ; but the fact that the Combes Cabinet was able to carry it out virtually unchallenged showed the enormous amount of ground lost by the Church in public opinion.

It was scarcely possible that the Concordat should survive the enforcement of such legislation, but the break might have been postponed had it not been for the incidents that accompanied President Loubet's visit to the King of Italy in April 1904, and that led to the rupture of diplomatic relations with Rome that same year. A separation law was drafted and passed in 1905, came into operation on January 1st, 1906, and was virtually ratified by the electorate in the general election in 1906.

This law, which still officially governs the relations of Church and State in France, proclaimed the complete neutrality of the State in matters of religion ; it abolished all State subsidies to religious bodies, who were left entirely free to manage their own affairs. In practice, it meant that the Pope could appoint bishops, and bishops parish clergy, without any need for governmental confirmation ; that priests and bishops were now free to express themselves on political matters without any fear of being prosecuted before the Conseil d'état for utterances incompatible with their position as civil servants. It did in fact place the Roman Catholic Church in France entirely under papal control : and would, therefore, have been in many ways hailed with joy by the ultramontane party had it not been for the unsatisfactory arrangement made by the law for the disposal of such fabric—churches, manses, seminaries—as had hitherto belonged to the State. These arrangements, which virtually placed Church property in the hands of lay bodies, was rejected by the Church as incompatible with her fundamental principles. The position of Catholics had therefore to be settled by a series of emergency measures which handed over all buildings to the commune; the faithful were left free to use the buildings for worship, but no provision was made from any funds for the upkeep. It was a very lame solution : several schemes for a more permanent settlement have been discussed, but so far all in vain.[1]

§ 2. *The ' Bloc' and the New Parties* [2]

It is now time to indicate how parties came into existence out of the struggles of the period just described. It was in 1898 that the ' Die-hard ' supporters of Church and Army, some royalists, some Bonapartists, and some ' republican plebiscitaries ',[3] i. e. all believers in some form of autocracy, monarchical, imperial, or dictatorial, formed the ' Ligue de la Patrie française '. Its platform was that of ' Nationalism ', France for the truly French,

---

[1] For a discussion of the present legal position of the Church, see Paul Bureau, *Quinze ans de séparation* (1906–21).
[2] See for this section Jacques, *Les Partis Politiques sous la Troisième République* (1912).
[3] For a fuller discussion of this standpoint, see ch. vi.

not for Jews, Protestants, and other ' métèques ' ; no
radicalism ; hostility to the democratic principles of
1789, and a jingo programme in foreign policy.[1] After
a very few years it became merged in a new organization,
the Ligue de l'Action française, which kept the whole
of the Nationalist programme but added to it the dogma
of absolute monarchy.   The League rallied round it,
however, many non-royalists who were dissatisfied with
Parliamentarism, and has exercised since its formation
an influence out of proportion to its membership, largely
owing to the singular literary talent of its chief promoters,
Charles Maurras, Léon Daudet, Jacques Bainville.

About the same time as the Ligue de la Patrie française
there came into existence an organization which under
the somewhat deceiving name of ' Action Libérale
Populaire ' sought to unite in defence of the Church
those who wanted to separate her from a programme of
political reaction.   Most of its members, led by the
Comte Albert de Mun, one of the noblest figures of the
last forty years, may be said to be monarchical at heart
but to have accepted the Republic as an inevitable fact ;
and instead of working for an impossible Restoration they
are concentrating their energies upon securing freedom
for a Church that would cease to play an important part
in party politics, and a greater freedom for the individual
from the influence of a State that professes complete
religious neutrality.   They are, therefore, Liberals in
so far as they are hostile to collectivism, and popular
in so far as they do not deny the fundamental principles
of democracy, but as a matter of fact their general action
is on very conservative lines and freedom for the Church
really sums up their policy.   They are to be carefully
distinguished from the ' Action Française ' party, partly
through their acceptance of the Republic but more
especially by their difference of attitude on ecclesiastical
matters, the ' Action Française ' being only favourable
to the Church in so far as it stands for the Crown and for
order, but repudiating its moral and dogmatic teaching :

[1] See Mr. H. A. L. Fisher's paper on ' French Nationalism ' in his
Studies of Politics and History. M. Barrès defines a Nationalist as
' a Frenchman who has a conscious realization of his formation '.

Charles Maurras has described himself as ' un catholique athée '.[1] ' L'Action Libérale Populaire ', on the other hand, is a genuinely Catholic body.

These two parties represent the extreme Conservative resistance to the general lines of Republican tradition and of course to the Bloc's policy. They could not in fact co-operate with any Republican group, and were consequently, until the great war, entirely outside ministerial combinations.

The forming of these extreme Conservative organizations made it necessary for the Republicans to adopt a similar policy and organize. The Radicals were the first to do so, by the fusion in 1901 of Radicals and Socialist Radicals into one party, the real basis of the ' Bloc ', the name given to the co-operation of all groups of the ' Left ' in the attack on the Church. Anti-clericalism was, of course, and still is their chief plank : but they also held to the old Radical ideas, as put forward by Gambetta in 1869 and re-expressed in 1907 at their congress at Nancy : State control of industry, nationalization of mines and railways, a progressive income-tax, and a pacifist foreign policy.[2]

Not all Radicals, however, joined the new organization. There were some who, while accepting anti-clericalism, disliked the collectivist programme of the Radical Socialists. They found a common basis of action with some Progressives who were profoundly dissatisfied with the attitude of their party during the Dreyfus crisis. These two elements joined to form in 1902 the Democratic Republican Alliance, which, while disclaiming the name of a party, virtually adopted the Radical programme in anti-clericalism and the Progressive opposition to anything savouring of Socialism ;[3] they became ultimately the dominant element in the 1919 Parliament. The

[1] ' It is one of the philosophical honours of the Church . . . to have set the verses of the *Magnificat* to a music that attenuates its poison ' (Maurras, *Le Chemin du Paradis*).

[2] For a detailed analysis of the pre-war Radical programme, see Jacques, op. cit. We agree with this writer that Radicalism is as much a temperament as a political creed.

[3] They declared their hostility to ' Nationalist anti-semitism and to revolutionary anarchy ' (Jacques).

remainder of the Progressives, faithful to the old policy
of anti-Socialism [1] and freedom for the Church, formed
themselves in 1903 into the Republican Federation. In
1910, some Radicals, favourable to collectivism but weary
of extreme anti-clericalism and hostile to pacificism, formed
the ' Republican Socialist Party '—a small organization
noteworthy for the large number it contained of men of
Cabinet rank. With this exception, the parties of to-day
were thus formed during the fight of the Radicals with
the Church and around the Radical anti-clerical and
collectivist programme.

On the other side, the Radical Socialists failed to
achieve a definite union with Jaurès and his followers.
It came to be realized on both sides that on matters of
industrial and international organization, which were
becoming increasingly important now that the anti-
clerical programme had been carried through, there was
no real harmony between Radical and Socialist policy.
Outside France, the tendency of Socialists was everywhere to concentrate and unite against all other parties,
and the Socialist Congress held at Amsterdam in 1904
finally condemned co-operation with bourgeois parties.
A final choice had to be made : MM. Millerand and
Viviani left the party, but the majority, including Jaurès
and Briand, decided to accept the decision of the Congress.
The division between them and the Guesdistes, therefore,
disappeared, and the two Socialist parties united into the
' United Socialist Party ', ' a class party, aiming at the
socialization of the means of production and distribution :
not a party of reform, but a party of class and revolution,
united against all bourgeois groups and bound to refuse
military credits, secret funds, credits for colonial expedi-
tions, and the budget as a whole ' (April 1905).   The
dissidents helped to form a few years later the Republican
Socialist party, to which reference has already been made ;
while the United Socialists, standing quite alone at the
next elections, won sweeping successes—58 seats in 1906,
75 in 1910, 101 in 1914.

[1] Mainly in nationalization and income-tax.

§ 3. *New Issues: Syndicalism and Foreign Affairs*

The re-forming of political parties upon lines of definite political action seemed to give more stability to political life. The violence of M. Combes's attack on the Church did lead indeed in 1905 to a temporary drawing back on the part of some of his followers, so that he was defeated and his Ministry replaced by two successive mixed Cabinets under MM. Rouvier and Sarrien. But this set-back to Radicalism was only temporary and was not confirmed by the general elections of 1906, in which Conservatives and Progressives lost heavily while the Radical groups found themselves with a practically homogeneous majority. It seemed as if France was entering upon a phase of yet fuller Radicalism, and the Clémenceau Cabinet, formed as a result of the election, put forward an ambitious programme : the income-tax, an eight-hour day, old age pensions, more freedom for Trade Unions and professional syndicates, increased State control over mines, State purchase of the Western Railway Company, electoral and administrative reforms, complete State monopoly of elementary education. But as it turned out, party and ministry were not as strong as they seemed : at the very start the new Parliament largely discredited itself in public opinion by the hasty voting in a virtually secret session of an increase in the stipend of deputies and senators from 9,000 to 15,000 francs.[1] Then it soon became evident that the unity of the majority was more apparent than real : a conflict with the General Federation of Labour showed the party to be seriously divided.

The Syndicalist movement, of which the *Confédération Générale du Travail* is the organ, must be as carefully distinguished from the Socialist party as Trade Unionism from the Labour party in England. In its early stages, indeed, French Trade Unionism was frankly socialistic, and we saw that the forming of the first Socialist party was the outcome of a Trade Union Congress held in 1879. By the end of the nineteenth century, however, while Socialists under Jaurès and Millerand were increasingly ' reformist ', i. e. believers in Parliamentary action and

---

[1] This is now 27,000 francs.

in the establishment of Socialism by the gradual absorp-
tion by the State of the organs of production and distribution, a reaction appeared in the Syndicalist theory
advanced by M. Georges Sorel, and soon adopted by the
greater number of Trade Union leaders—namely that the
duty of the workers is ' to destroy the existing political
organization and to deprive the State and all local
authorities of all their functions in order to transfer them
to the Trade Unions '.[1]   The methods by which this new
system was to be ushered in were those of direct action—
strikes, boycotts, and sabotage.

Whether or not this theory was, as M. Sorel claimed,
but a logical deduction from Marxism, there was obviously
much in common between this programme and that of
the Marxist Socialists, and when they became the dominant
factor in the reunited Socialist party, about the same
time as the General Confederation of Labour definitely
adopted Syndicalism (1905–6), the difference between the
Socialist party and the Confederation became one of
organization rather than one of policy or principles.
There remained some Socialist deputies who were not
Syndicalist in their sympathies, and a few Syndicalists
who did not vote for Socialist candidates, but both bodies
represented much the same tendencies, the destruction by
revolutionary methods of the capitalist society, and the
entire elimination of political frontiers by the international
action of the proletariat.

The definite adoption of Syndicalism by the C. G. T.,
as the Confederation is usually called, threw French
industrial life into a condition of turmoil and confusion,
manifested by an endless series of strikes : Paris electri-
cians, grocers' assistants, naval workers, Paris builders,
wine-growers in the south.

It was on the attitude to be adopted towards Syndicalism and in particular towards strikers that the Radicals
became divided.   Clémenceau and the Cabinet believed
in firm repression, and troops were called in to restore
order among the wine-growers.   One of the regiments
concerned mutinied.   A considerable number of Radicals
were hostile to repressive measures and voted with the

[1] Dell, *My Second Country*, p. 255.

Socialists against the Government, which was only kept in office by Conservative votes.   The break between ministerial Radicals and Socialists was in fact the opening of a new chapter in party politics.   An attempt made by the Union of Elementary Teachers to be recognized as part of the General Workers' Federation caused a further conflict : a Postal Workers' strike widened the breach, and by the beginning of 1909 the Radical Bloc was in pieces : the Clémenceau Cabinet fell in July.   M. Briand formed his first Cabinet with the greater number of Clémenceau's ministers, and carried on until the elections of 1910 in which the old divisions into smaller groups appeared once more.   The results were vague : the Socialists undoubtedly gained about twenty seats, but while the nominal distribution of seats among other groups remained much the same, so many new members entered the House and party labels were washing so colourless that it was very difficult to make any accurate calculations.

The same questions which had divided the last Chamber soon appeared.   The Briand Cabinet had to deal in the summer with a railway strike, and its repression finally broke the last links between Radicals and Socialists. The Government was now liable to constant attacks both from the Right and the Left ; and the new Parliament was going to ' use up ' no less than eight Cabinets.   A re-modelling of the ministry on slightly more radical lines in November 1910 did not disarm the Socialists, and M. Briand had to retire in February 1911.   A new Radical Cabinet under M. Monis, including as finance minister M. Caillaux, the income-tax champion, only lived three months.   Caillaux himself remade the ministry (June 1911).

Ministerial instability and party incoherence were increased by the introduction in 1910 of a new issue that cut across ordinary party divisions, Proportional Representation.   As this tended to give more adequate representation to minorities, the Radicals, then in office, inclined to be hostile and the opposition parties favourable. But many changed sides, and the ministers themselves were no longer united.   The Caillaux Cabinet, however, definitely accepted the principle of the reform, and the struggle became chiefly a matter of methods. It would probably have passed under Caillaux had it not been for the fall of the ministry in January 1912, over the Premier's foreign policy of conciliation with Germany. From this moment till now, foreign and military affairs have been the dominant issue and tend even now to overshadow internal politics. It was mainly over national security against the foreigner that a Poincare Ministry was then formed. The new Cabinet proposed no reforms save proportional representation, but 'was determined to assume all responsibilities, to exercise firmly all authority, to maintain public peace and to repress crime '. The new tendencies of the Chamber were expressed by the election of a Conservative Speaker (M. Deschanel), and a few months later by the election of the Premier to the Presidency of the Republic. Immediately after, proportional representation shared the fate of the income-tax : it was thrown out by the Senate (March 1913). M. Briand, who had succeeded M. Poincaré, resigned, and the Chamber let the Cabinet go rather than open a conflict with the Upper House.

A new Cabinet was formed by M. Barthou, who, as minister for war in the previous ministry, had brought forward a proposal that was to dwarf all other issues and to go a long way towards reuniting Radicals and Socialists. He demanded the lengthening of the period of military service from two to three years. This was a return to the system prevailing between 1889 and 1905, but at that time many categories of young men served for one year only. The Radicals had equalized conditions in 1905 by making the period two years for all without any exception : the new scheme was for three years, also without any exceptions. The Opposition was very violent, and reunited Socialists under Jaurès and the Radicals hostile to the new measure under Caillaux.[1] The result was the fall of the ministry as soon as the measure had been voted (December

[1] In January 1914, at the Amiens Socialist Congress, Jaurès urged that Socialists should co-operate on second ballots with ' candidates of other parties hostile to the three-year law, jingoism and the military-clerical reaction '. This was obviously a reference to the Caillaux

1913). The new Cabinet included Caillaux [1] but did not propose the immediate repeal of the law, its intention being to appeal to the country at the 1914 general election. But events made this impossible. The anti-ministerial Radicals, Briand, Millerand, Barthou, formed a new anti-Radical union called the Federation of the Left, with the object of forming a Republican anti-Radical Bloc. Against this, Socialists and ministerial Radicals prepared a common platform : return to two years' service law, income-tax, no church schools. Just before the elections, however, the Radical leader had to retire from political life and his policy unavoidably suffered ; but the elections scarcely weakened the Radicals, and when the Doumergue Cabinet retired, owing to the disappearance of its real head, moderates were unable to form a Cabinet, and a Radical Ministry was formed under a Republican Socialist, Viviani, who declared in favour of income-tax and was silent about the three-year law, which would almost certainly have been repealed, had not the war then broken out. [2]

Radicals. M. Paix-Séailles, in *Jaurès et Caillaux*, describes the gradual drawing together of the two politicians between 1911 and 1914.

[1] M. Doumergue was Prime Minister. Caillaux's unpopularity with the Conservatives and Progressives made it impossible for him to lead the Cabinet, of which he was the virtual head.

[2] ' On the eve of the war, with the Three Years' Service Act as the main issue, French politics seemed to be concentrating into something that had a temporary resemblance to the two-party system. The Left was gaining something like the cohesion and the discipline of an English party, and at its head, with his hand on provincial organizations, on finance and on the press, as well as on the Parliamentary groups, was M. Caillaux. Wealth, the power of work, a grasp of detail, and above all an unusual courage, had given him a power common enough in Great Britain but rare in France. The Briands, the Millerands, the Vivianis, were orators and tacticians ; he was a party leader in the English sense. . . . At bottom, we believe it was largely the French dread of a citizen who becomes too powerful which led to his arrest. . . . There was something of the same dread of ascendancy in the murder of Jaurès.' *The Nation*, Jan. 24, 1922. Without endorsing this appreciation of M. Caillaux's personal qualities, we believe this is a true analysis of political conditions in 1914.

CHAPTER V

PARTY EVOLUTION SINCE 1914

§ 1. *Parties during the War*

THE ' Sacred Union ' of all parties that was immediately proclaimed was not very long-lived. Although party differences as such might be forgotten, personal animosities remained. There were consequently several changes of Cabinet during the war : M. Viviani resigned in October 1915 and was succeeded by M. Briand. He in turn gave place to M. Ribot in March 1917. M. Ribot only remained in office for six months and was succeeded by the even shorter-lived Painlevé Cabinet ; finally in November 1917 M. Clémenceau formed the ministry that was to carry the war to its close and to make the treaty of Versailles. Apart from the fact that the Clémenceau Cabinet included no Socialists and, save the Prime Minister himself, no advanced Radicals, those changes mean little in the history of French party politics ; they represent mainly impatience at the slowness of the war's progress, an attempt to find the man who would make adequate use of the nation's resources or discover a short cut to victory.[1]

Taken as a whole, however, the war undoubtedly weakened the Radicals and strengthened the Conservatives. Those who had been warning the nation of the German peril and had advocated military preparation and a spirited foreign policy were apparently confirmed by facts, and their opponents discredited. Those who during the war had expressed their willingness to accept a less decisive peace than that ultimately signed at Versailles were derided as ' defeatists ', while Caillaux, who had believed the war could be avoided by a new departure in foreign policy, had forfeited public esteem by the scandals of his private life, and had adopted during the war an attitude so suspicious that he was arrested on

[1] It is impossible to enter here into the vexed question of the influence of party politics on the conduct of the war, particularly in appointments to high commands in the army.

a charge of treason ; and although he was acquitted on this grave count he was found guilty of correspondence with the enemy and banished for ten years.[1]

The effects of the war upon the Socialist party deserve to be studied more closely. The mass of French Socialists, deprived of their leader by the murder of Jaurès on July 31, began by supporting the Government, Guesde and Sembat accepting portfolios in Viviani's reconstructed Cabinet of national defence. But differences soon appeared, some declaring their belief that the war was a war of capitalists with which the proletariat were not concerned and that the Allies' war aims were really as 'imperialist' as those of the Germans. This minority, led by Jean Longuet, a grandson of Karl Marx, did not at once refuse war credits, but began by demanding a statement of Peace aims and advocated an early termination of the war on lines approaching the *status quo ante bellum*. But this minority soon split into two groups, a small fraction, led by Raffin-Dugens and Brizon, voting against war credits and attending at Zimmerwald and Keinthal international congresses at which German Socialists were present.

The rapid growth of the minority elements is the striking feature of the next few years. While in December 1915 they could only muster 76 votes in the party's congress as against 2,376, in April 1916 Longuet's motion to resume relations with German Socialists obtained 960 votes (against 1,996), and in December 1916 the co-operation of Albert Thomas as minister of munitions in the Briand Cabinet was only allowed by 1,637 votes to 1,372. By the Spring of 1917 the minority was becoming a majority : in May the party voted the participation in the Stockholm conference : in September M. Thomas had to leave the Painlevé Cabinet, and the continuation of war credits was only voted in November 1917 by 1,552 to 1,334 votes. Finally in July 1918 the Longuet motion demanding the definition of war aims and refusing to vote war credits unless passports were granted for an international conference was voted by 1,690 to

[1] One of Caillaux's lieutenants, Malvy, Minister of the Interior in the first war Cabinet, was banished for five years on a similar charge.

1,172. As a result the *Humanité*, the party's official organ, passed into the hands of the new majority.

To study in detail the causes of this change would take us too far afield. The constant postponing of the trial of Vilain, the murderer of Jaures, undoubtedly exasperated Socialist opinion ; it was alleged that the trial would stir up party strife and, therefore, disturb the ' Sacred Union ', but no effects on party cohesion could have been as serious as the fact that the postponement of the trial for five years and the subsequent acquittal of the murderer led Socialists—and many others—to believe that to a bourgeois society the murder of a Socialist leader for political reasons was a matter of little importance. The strictness of the censorship in refusing to allow the statement, or even the discussion, of war aims, all these were contributory factors to the abandonment by the Socialists of their support of the war. But the real direct cause was the Russian revolution. The Socialists had always been critical of the alliance of the French Republic with Russian autocracy, and thought the downfall of Tsarism should be hailed with joy. They were irritated by the dismay with which the western powers greeted the advent of Socialists to power under Kerensky, and by their refusal to adopt his motto of a peace without indemnities or annexations. Finally the open hostility shown by the Allies to the Bolshevist revolution inevitably drove the Marxists of France into open opposition to the war, and led to the adoption by the Congresses held in Paris in April 1919 of motions declaring the complete restoration of the class struggle, unreconcilable opposition to bourgeois ministries, the pursuit of a social revolution according to the example of Russia, Hungary, and Germany, and the entering upon ' fraternal relations ' with the Moscow International.

§ 2. *The Elections of 1919*

While the Socialists had completely broken off their relations with the bourgeois parties, these parties were finding on the other hand that many of their former differences were disappearing in their unity on greater issues, such as national defence, foreign policy, and hostility to the domestic and international programme of the Socialists. Many party leaders thought, therefore, that a return to party conflicts was premature, and endeavoured to find for all Republican parties a common platform of national reconstruction, of which the chief planks were the maintenance of the treaty of Versailles and ' anti-Bolshevism '.

The formation of this ' National Bloc ' was largely the work of the Democratic Alliance, which became the leading element of the movement ; the Republican Federation, the Republican Socialists, the Liberal Action, and a certain number of Radicals adhered, but not the Radical Socialist party as such.

The victory of the Bloc was complete. Both the Democratic Alliance and the Liberal Action doubled their representation (from 77 to 133, and from 32 to 69), while that of the Republican Federation was increased fourfold (from 36 to 133). On the other hand the Radicals lost 114 of their 257 seats and the Socialists 33 of their 101. Taken as a whole, the Bloc returned over 400 members out of a total of 610, nearly two-thirds of the members of the 1914 Parliament losing their seats. The final result was to give France one of the most Conservative Chambers she has ever had.[1]

That these results were a fair indication of the change in public opinion can scarcely be questioned, but the method of election adopted undoubtedly tended to over-emphasize the effects of the ' swing of the pendulum '. By a law passed in July 1919 a return was made to the multiple-member constituency, in which votes are cast for a whole list : with this was combined a curious system of proportional representation, of which the virtual result was to suppress the representation of minorities. Under this scheme any candidate receiving a clear majority of the votes actually expressed is elected. If therefore a party-list is able to win a bare majority of the electorate, the whole list is elected.

[1] In the Senatorial elections held in January 1920, the Conservatives gained 5 seats, the ' Bloc ' parties 25, the Socialists 2, the Republican Socialists 2. The Radicals lost 16 seats.

The results were curious. Here and there undoubtedly a small party was able to win an odd seat which it never would have obtained under the single-member system : for instance, the ' Action Francaise ' party returned five members, whereas they had none in the previous Parliaments. But the Socialists lost, as we saw, one-third of their 101 seats, whereas they actually polled 300,000 more votes than in 1914 (1,700,000 to 1,400,000). The election in the fourth district of Paris, where the Socialists polled a total of 1,576,602 against the Bloc's poll of 2,102,411, is typical. Under any ordinary system of proportional representation the Socialists would have received 6 out of the 14 seats balloted for ; or had the district been divided into 14 single-member constituencies they would have been very unlucky if they had not obtained a majority in at least 3 or 4. But under the scheme in operation they did not get a single seat.

The elections were therefore to some extent misleading, and divisions appeared as soon as the new Parliament formed itself into its customary groups. Any hopes that the Bloc would retain even an outward unity were soon dashed to the ground.

§ 3.   *Party Divisions in the present Parliament*

We have already said that parliamentary groups are quite distinct from the parties, and may even cut across party divisions.[1] It often happens that a party contains several leaders who on personal grounds find it impossible to work together happily ; or that a number of deputies from several parties unite in support of a particular measure or of a restricted programme. This is the case in the present Chamber with a group called ' Republican and Social Action ', which is formed by the uniting of some 46 members on a non-party programme of social reform ; its leader is M. Bokanowski.

The strictly party groups are as follows :

1. The ' Republican Democratic Entente ', led by M. Arago, contains nearly all the Republican Federation

---

[1] For a discussion of the system, see Finer, ' The Group System in France,' *Economica*, January 1921.

and the Right (anti-Radical) wing of the Democratic Alliance. It may well become the basis of a reconstructed Progressive party. Its membership is 183, and it is the largest group in the House.

2. The ' Republican Democratic Left ' unites the middle fraction of the Democratic Alliance and a number of other Progressives unable to co-operate with the Entente. It numbers 93 members, and is led by M. Barthou.

3. The ' Republicans of the Left ' comprise the remnant of the Democratic Alliance, with a few Progressives and some moderate Radicals ; among its chief men is M. Tardieu, the man who most nearly represents M. Clémenceau's policy. It numbers 61.

It will be noticed that while these three groups all include members of three parties, the Republican Federation, the Democratic Alliance, and the Liberal Action, none of the groups contains the whole membership of any one party. Nor can the ' Independents ', as the extreme Conservatives call themselves, be said to form a party. To find any correspondence between party and group we have to go to the opposition side, where we find the 86 Radical Socialists, presided over by M. Herriot, and the 26 Republican Socialists, under M. Painlevé, corresponding to the parties of those names. And it should be noticed that the Radical group only contains just over half the members elected on the party ticket.

The four Cabinets formed since the Chamber met have all contained members of all the Republican groups, excluding only the Monarchical and Socialist parties. It is indeed typical of the confusion of French party politics that the Poincaré Cabinet, formed as a revolt against M. Briand's foreign policy, should contain twelve members of M. Briand's Cabinet, and be recruited among virtually the same political groups.[1] But it would be completely

[1] The Poincaré Cabinet is made up as follows :
Senatorial ministers : 2 from the Democratic Left : MM. Poincaré (Prime Minister and Foreign Affairs) and Chéron (Agriculture).
2 from the Republican Entente : MM. Peyronnet (Labour) and Strauss (Hygiene).
Deputy ministers : 5 from the Democratic Left : MM. Barthou (Justice), Bérard (Education), Maunoury (Interior), Maginot (War), Colrat (Under Secretary).

misleading to conclude that either the Briand or the
Poincaré Cabinets possessed the virtually unanimous
support of the Chamber.   Several of these ministers
joined the ministry against the advice of their group
leaders, whereas certain groups who did not obtain or
wish for any seats in the Cabinet usually support it.   The
clearest thing will be to show how the parties voted over
the general vote of confidence given to the new Cabinet.

All the Socialists (64), 5 Republican Socialists, 8 Radical
Socialists, and 7 Independents voted against ; while
12 Republican Socialists, 53 Radical Socialists, 4 members
of the Democratic Left, 5 members of the Republican
and Social Action, 1 member of the Republican Entente,
and 3 Independents abstained from voting.   The Cabinet
has therefore at present the virtually unanimous support
of the Right, Centre, and Left Centre parties : it is opposed
by the mass of the three parties that claim to be Socialist,
and this line of division seems likely to represent fairly
accurately the present political situation.   The vote of
confidence was supported by 434 votes, out of 615
deputies ; this is just about equal to the National Bloc,
and the vote shows that the Bloc stands solid in matters
of foreign policy and in hostility towards Socialism.

§ 4.   *Present-day Problems* [1]

It is unnecessary to discuss here the foreign policy of
France since the armistice.   Countless articles on the
subject have appeared in the English press, representing
every standpoint from fulsome and blind eulogy to bitter
and equally blind hostility.   Putting aside controversial
issues, it is, however, possible to insist upon a few facts
that may help to a better understanding of a difficult

[3] from the Republican Entente : MM. Dior (Commerce), Lasteyrie
(Finance), Raiberti (Navy).

[2] Republicans of the Left : MM. Eynac (Air), le Trocquer (Public
Works).

[2] Republican Socialists : MM. Rio and Vidal (both Under Secretaries).

[2] Radicals : MM. Laffont (Post Office), Sarraut (Colonies).

[1] from the Republican and Social Action : M. Reibel (liberated
regions).

[1] The attitude of the Government towards Socialism and Syndicalism
will best be dealt with when we discuss the present position of those
movements in the next chapter.

situation. The first is that Germany, however complete her military and economic collapse, has still got her industrial machinery intact and a population considerably in excess of that of France. The French, whose territory has twice within half a century been invaded by a professedly pacific neighbour, are still living in the fear engendered by those invasions and by their numerical inferiority ; they declare they cannot trust the pacific professions of the present German Government, and that they must make up for their deficiency in numbers by keeping under arms a force considerably in excess of that allowed to Germany by the Peace Treaty. They maintain that they can count on no one besides themselves, since Great Britain, in consequence of America's refusal, declined to enter into a pact on the promise of which France gave up her claims to the Rhine as a permanent military frontier. 'As to the League of Nations,' says M. Poincaré, ' it can render great services to humanity, . . . but it is unfortunately unable to give France those guarantees she needs.' [1]

At the present moment, the French Government propose a period of military service of eighteen months, thanks to which they can keep up an army of about 420,000 men (including 80,000 native troops), as against German forces, which they estimate at 250,000. ' We must disarm ', said the chairman of the Parliamentary Commission on the Army Law, ' proportionally with Germany, but keeping always at a distance from her that will give us an evident advantage and guarantee the fruits of victory, our security and our right to reparations.' [2]

The enforcement of reparations, for which this army may be needed, brings in a second essential factor of the situation. Without German money France is virtually bankrupt. ' If Germany does not pay, the problem is insoluble,' said the chairman of the Budget Commission in the Senate a year ago.[3] Even before the war few

[1] *Revue des Deux Mondes*, Chronique politique, Dec. 1st, 1921.
[2] Quoted in the *Temps*, March 4, 1922. A resolution for a one-year period of service was only defeated, however, by 83 votes, which shows that many Frenchmen consider the above establishment to be in excess of the real needs of France.
[3] Quoted in the *Revue des Deux Mondes*, April 15, 1921.

budgets balanced normally, and financial expedients were frequent, the Conservative parties being unanimous in opposing the income-tax as involving an unwarrantable interference with the private affairs of individuals. The necessities of the war broke down this resistance, but although France has now a fairly high income-tax, evasion of the tax is easy and widespread, and public opinion scarcely tolerates the alleged inquisitorial methods by which such evasion can be repressed. A drastic revision in her expenditure and her methods of collecting revenue must be one of the chief preoccupations of her ministers for some years to come. It is indeed probable that party conflicts will rage over those matters, Radicals and Socialists being in favour of a heavier income-tax, and even discussing the possibility of a capital levy—a scheme which would probably raise an even more violent opposition than in this country, owing to the immense number of small investors in State funds.

Finance and reparations are therefore inseparable problems, and these two are only part of the greater issue, which is the question of Franco-German relations and the maintenance of the Treaty of Versailles. The matter of Germany's capacity to pay is one of life and death to France ; even the cancellation of her debt to the Allies would not solve the problem ; and it is not unnatural that on this point even the Radicals should be behind M. Poincaré's Cabinet in his insistence on the enforcement of the reparations clauses. Differences of opinion centre more round the best method of obtaining these payments, and particularly around the larger question of the influence of reparations payments on the economic reconstruction of Europe as a whole. It is probably not inaccurate to say that the conclusions laid down by Mr. J. M. Keynes would be adopted by the Radicals and disputed by the government parties. Further, the opposition is inclined to the belief that Germany is sincere in her professions of peace, and that the German military peril is largely the result of an over-excited imagination ; they are therefore hostile to the maintenance of even an eighteen months military service, and favour the adoption of a militia system, on the lines of the Swiss, as suggested before the war by Jaurès.[1]

Finance is therefore the ultimate key to present foreign policy, and the present position can only be understood when it is realized that the alternative to payment by Germany is a financial policy so drastic as to amount almost to a social revolution. The necessity for a choice is growing every day more apparent, hence the increasing bitterness of the conflict between Government and Opposition.

The solution of post-war problems is thus bringing once more to the front pre-war issues and divisions. The old dispute of clericalism has been reopened over the re-establishment of diplomatic relations with the Papacy, the breaking-off of which in 1904 was the first step towards disestablishment. The government proposals for sending once more an ambassador to the Vatican aroused the hostility of the anti-clerical members of the Democratic Alliance as well as of the Radicals, and although the measure passed in both Houses, it perilously escaped defeat in the Senate (by 116 to 125 votes). Just over a year ago an interpellation in the Chamber over the Government's general home policy produced a curiously mixed resolution by which the House expressed its equal condemnation of ' collectivist doctrines, bolshevist propaganda, and clerical and royalist manœuvres' (menées), showing that even the National Bloc must pay at least lip-service to the old tradition of anti-clericalism.[2]

It is to be hoped, nevertheless, that the Cabinet will seize the opportunity of a Parliament in which extremists are in a minority to find some solution for the still unsettled matter of ecclesiastical property, and that some form of ownership may be devised that will be acceptable both to the Church and to those who still support the essential principle of the Separation Law. This would do

---

[1] M. Hennessy, one of the Radical-Socialist leaders, accuses the Government of being ' inspired by imperialistic visions ', and of ' forgetting Republican traditions' in foreign affairs. Manifesto of the ' Ligue de la République', in l'Europe Nouvelle, February 1922. See also a recent speech by M. Jouhaux, Secretary of the General Confederation of Labour, quoted in the French Press of March 1st, 1922.

[2] See the Temps, December 24, 1920.

much to allay the 'intense religious bitterness' which Lord Bryce saw in the France of 1914 and which the war may have abated but has certainly not removed.

Religious issues of a yet more controversial character, however, seem likely to be raised. The Catholics are not unnaturally anxious if not actually to repeal, at least to mitigate, the harsh laws which ordered the closing of all schools staffed by members of religious orders, and the return to France of Alsace and Lorraine makes the subject all the more pressing, as those two provinces have kept during the half-century of German rule the Concordat and the laws allowing denominational schools. The anti-clericals are anxious to bring these provinces into line with the rest of France, but this is strenuously resisted by Alsatian Catholics, some of whom have threatened to appeal to the League of Nations should any attempt be made to deprive them of their religious liberty ; while the Catholics in the rest of France urge that the reunion to France of those Catholics should bring about a general relaxation of the present anti-clerical system.

The problems we have just discussed seem likely to occupy the remainder of the present legislature and to be the dominant issues at the next elections. Those who were hoping that the Bloc National would be able, owing to its large majority, to carry out a positive programme of national and economic reconstruction and prove sufficiently homogeneous to give a long life to a non-party Cabinet have seen their expectations disappointed. This failure may have been due to inherent defects in its composition—its enemies accuse it of being only a re-actionary manœuvre, based on the deliberate exaggeration of Bolshevist danger ; it may have failed by reason of its very breadth ; it might have been better frankly to ignore the Radical groups and govern only with the Centre and the Right, without having to make any concessions to the Left. At the time of writing (May 1922) it is too early to see whether M. Poincaré will be able to carry out a more continuous policy than his predecessors. We doubt it, because it seems to us that the Bloc from its birth was in a false position. It assumed that it could confine itself to questions of foreign policy and of economic, financial, and social reconstruction, and keep silent about internal politics on which it was not united ; but anti-Bolshevism is not a programme, and party politics have an uncomfortable knack of appearing at awkward moments and refusing to be shelved. In an article of December 1920, dealing with parties and programmes, the *Temps* refers to the need of putting finance on a sound basis, of returning to normal budgets, of rebuilding the devastated regions, and of opposing to communist propaganda ' positive social accomplishments '. It is an unfortunate fact that none of these issues are free from political implications or from the pressure of financial interests that are scarcely distinguishable from political reaction. The Bloc was an experiment, foredoomed to failure for ignoring the fundamental reality of party divisions.

CHAPTER VI

PRESENT STRENGTH OF FRENCH PARTIES

THE war does not appear to have disturbed the general classification into four main parties which we made at the beginning of our study. What it has done is to reinforce certain lines of division and to effect others, and particularly to alter very considerably the balance of power among them.[1]

§ 1. *Royalists, Bonapartists, and ' Caesarists '*

The Royalist party only needs a brief mention. Reference has already been made to their chief agency, the ' Ligue de l'Action Francaise '. As an active ferment it has to be reckoned with : it was largely instrumental in establishing the Clémenceau Ministry in November 1917 and in overthrowing M. Briand last January. It has wealthy supporters, commands the services of some of

---

[1] See for this whole chapter : Guy-Grand, *Le conflit des idées dans la France d'aujourd'hui* (1921), a remarkable study of the political psychology of contemporary France.

the most able pens in the country, and is extremely
' vocal ', but it has little following outside the aristocracy
and a small section of the Catholic bourgeoisie ; and it
would be a great mistake to conclude from the influence
the party wields that the restoration of the old royal
house is within the sphere of practical politics.

The reinstatement of the Bonapartes is even less likely
than that of the Bourbons ; but if as an organized party
Bonapartism is very weak, for the memories of Sedan
will not readily disappear, the force of the general principles which the two emperors represented, or professed to
represent, cannot be ignored in a study of contemporary
France.   Bonapartism is not merely allegiance to a
dynasty : it is an attitude of mind.[1]   It stands for the
idea that the best form of government is the absolute
rule of a democratically selected autocrat.   It is, it may
be said, an approximation to the American system of
presidential government, but the American President
enjoys powers which, if large, are nevertheless defined by
law, and must be exercised concurrently with an elected
Parliament ;   whereas the supporters of ' La Monarchie
Plebiscitaire ', seizing upon the central fact of Napoleonic
rule, namely, that the Napoleons were virtual despots
who were able to ignore the machinery and restrictions
of representative institutions, really wish their sovereign
to be unhampered in any measures he may take for what
he conceives to be the national welfare.   Bonapartists
are therefore sworn foes of Parliamentarism, and their
main object is precisely to replace the rule of an assembly
by the rule of one man only bound to render account at
the end of his term of service.

It is evident that this conception need not be the
monopoly of one party, and there are in fact very few
Frenchmen who have not at some time been fascinated
by the vision of ' a despot . . . a beneficent despot,
naturally, a large-minded benevolent despot—in short,
a despot to obey their bidding ' ;[2]   and times of crisis
have always fanned into a flame the dormant enthusiasm

[1] See Barrès, *Les Déracinés*, ch. viii, and our article on ' The Napoleonic Legend in 1921 ' in the *Friends' Quarterly Examiner*, July 1921.
[2] Meredith, *Diana of the Crossways*.

of the masses for a leader of that type, so that whenever for a brief while the establishment of this dictatorship has seemed possible, men of widely divergent standpoints have been found united in hailing the advent of the *deus ex machina*. It is noteworthy that among the earliest supporters of Louis Napoleon Bonaparte in 1848 was such a sturdy Radical as Victor Hugo, and when 40 years later the Republic had to meet the attack of Boulangism, there were to be found among the partisans of the General some idealist Republicans who saw in him the hope of democracy. Ten years later, when a dictatorship seemed to some to be the only way out of the chaos of the Dreyfus affair, the bulk of Boulanger's former supporters wore the new label of ' Nationalists '; but the Republicans were now unitedly hostile, realizing that under the specious words of an appeal to the people, what was really desired was the shelving of representative institutions, the forcible silencing of all opposition, and the re-establishment of a despotism that would make short work of Republican idealism.

The fact is that ' Caesarism ', as the policy of dictatorship is usually called, has never succeeded in dismissing some of the worst traditions of pure Bonapartism—it has always stood for aggression abroad and for the repression of any organizations such as trade unions or political clubs which could voice an effective opposition. It has in a word always stood for order and the sword as against liberty and free speech. Even now, however, Caesarism can appeal to popular imagination, and the wave of enthusiasm which carried M. Clémenceau to office at the end of 1917, and made him the most powerful Prime Minister of Republican France, with a completely subservient Parliament and virtually absolute powers, was true to the Bonapartist traditions, while the refusal to the victorious Clémenceau of the obvious reward of the Presidency reveals another force of French political life, namely the Republican reluctance to entrust to any man for a long time powers which he might use for the overthrow of the Republic. The alleged mediocrity of most Presidents and Premiers is due to the fear that too strong a leader would easily appeal to this latent hero-worship and subvert the constitution to his own ends.

On the whole, the Caesarist tradition remains an incalculable but extremely important factor in French politics : a sudden outburst of popular dissatisfaction with the Parliamentary machine and of impatience with its obvious weaknesses, the coming into the limelight of some attractive figure, the discrediting of the leaders of the day through some scandal or conspicuous failure, might very well raise some popular hero to sudden and extraordinary power.[1]

§ 2. *The Republican Parties*

In France, as in England, the term ' conservative ' is used to describe the parties of the extreme Right, but it should really be applied to the moderate Republicans, to which the mass of the ' bourgeoisie ' belongs. They are truly conservative, in so far as to them certain events, certain institutions, are permanent acquisitions which nothing can disturb. The constitution of 1875 and the present economic organization have put political and social power into their hands, and neither must be touched. ' Neither reaction nor revolution ' is their motto ; and it may be said that they have really controlled the Third Republic : for many so-called Radicals belong to them by temperament and tradition. The present representation of the party in Parliament is a fair index of its real influence in the country. Its chief plank is perhaps allegiance to the existing economic framework of society and consequent hostility to Socialism or to any measure tampering with private property, such as nationalization, high income-tax or death duties, and

[1] We quote the following from the French press of June 15, 1921 : ' Following upon the centenary of Napoleon I, a group has just been formed under the name of " The National Party " for the advocacy in the present circumstances of the methods of order, foresight, and activity of the Napoleonic doctrine. The group repudiates any political aims and tends to the fusion of all parties, under the inspiration of this motto of Napoleon : to make the Republic beloved of its citizens, equitable to foreigners, and formidable to enemies. The programme of the party will be published later.'

syndicalism ; for it must be remembered that the mass of the peasant proprietors and the enormous number of small ' rentiers ', or people living on funds invested in State loans, would not tolerate any schemes subversive of that framework. But they will equally resist attacks from the Right : they tolerate the Church, considering it as a valuable guarantee of social stability, but are suspicious of clericalism ; they have no objection to a spirited foreign policy but are hostile to militarism or to expensive military adventures. They form in a word a useful bulwark against revolution, but have been not unjustly accused of narrowness of outlook and of a selfish opposition to essential social reforms. The party undoubtedly commands a clear majority in the present Parliament, and, could it formulate a clear policy, could form a homogeneous cabinet and carry the policy through. But its division into rival groups, the notorious personal differences between some of its leaders, and the general lack of party discipline, which is the bane of French politics, has so far caused that majority to be virtually helpless.

The other great Republican party, the Radicals, also claims the motto neither reaction nor revolution ', but interprets it differently. To a Socialist upheaval on the Russian model the Radicals are indeed hostile : but not to collectivism in general. They do not object, therefore, as do the Moderates, to considerable changes in the economic organization of society ; they are hostile to the power exerted at present by financial interests, and are virtually committed to the principle of a capital levy. In foreign affairs their attitude, without being exactly one of ' pacifism ', is the very negation of the nationalism of the Action Française and of some Conservatives ; they believed before the war, and many still do believe, that the co-operation of France and Germany resulting from a pacific settlement of their quarrels was as possible, and as essential to European peace, as the Entente Cordiale with Great Britain. And, above all, they are the party of extreme anti-clericalism ; and the great quarrel, the ' eternally alive ' Affaire Dreyfus, is the source of their inspiration and tradition. But anti-

clericalism, even if it be not a dead issue, is now but
a negative principle, and the criticism levelled at the
Radical party is that it has so far failed to evolve a
programme of action sufficiently distinct both from
Conservatism and from Socialism to warrant the continuation of the party as a separate body. Radicalism
is in fact very much in the same position as 'Independent
Liberalism' in this country; its enemies accuse it of
having no real life of its own, and of existing mainly on
the past reputation of a few personalities and on a programme made of a combination of defunct party cries
and of borrowings from the Socialists.[1] It would indeed
be easy to draw a close parallel between the present
attitude of both those parties on the main issues of the day.

In the present struggle between the Socialist and
bourgeois parties, the Radicals occupy a centre position
which is not easy to define, for they are looked upon with
suspicion by both sides, being equally opposed to the
system which the Socialists wish to establish and to the
methods which the Conservatives are prepared to use in
self-defence—such as the arbitrary dissolution of trade
unions, prosecutions for communist propaganda, and the
numerous other weapons provided by the administration.
The tendency to be found in certain quarters to divide
the political forces of the country into two only, Socialists
and anti-Socialists, fails to take into account the existence
of those who maintain that such a sharp division is both
unnecessary and undesirable.

No study of the present position of French Radicalism
would be complete without some reference to its leaders,
MM. Malvy and Caillaux. We saw how the condemnation
of these Radical ministers discredited the party during
the war and weakened it at the elections. If the sentence
passed on them was just, the Radical party should
deliberately repudiate them and make their return to
political life impossible. There are many indications,
however, that the Radicals believe Caillaux and Malvy

[1] The Radical 'Ligue de la République' states in its recent manifesto
that 'it recognizes as Republicans those who accept without qualifica-
tions the Republic as defined by Gambetta in his Belleville programme
of 1869' (see p. 28).

to have been condemned by political enemies as a revenge for their advocacy of the income-tax and of a Franco-German reconciliation. So far, no official pronouncement has been made on the subject ; but it seems that Radicalism will be helpless until it chooses between two courses—the expulsion from the party of two statesmen rightly condemned for disloyalty to the country, or a campaign for the clearing of their reputation and for the exposure of a judicial scandal as serious as the Affaire Dreyfus. There can be no middle way.[1]

§ 3. *Socialism and Syndicalism*

Since the war it is more than ever necessary to distinguish between these two movements, for they have not followed a parallel evolution : whereas we saw between 1902 and 1906 the C.G.T. gradually winning over the Socialist body to its revolutionary standpoint, we now see Socialism evolving more and more towards the extreme Left, while in the C.G.T. the moderate elements still hold their own.

We saw that the congress held in Paris in April 1919 marked the drawing yet nearer of Socialists to the Russian revolution, but not the actual linking of the party with the ' Third ' International. At a further congress, held in Strasburg in February 1920, the growth of extremist tendencies within the party was still more evident. Although the motion in favour of immediate union with Moscow was not carried, the congress adopted a resolution expelling from its membership those who were opposed to Bolshevist principles, and withdrawing from the ' Second ' International as being too

[1] The ' Ligue des Droits de l'Homme ' appears to have taken up the matter. Cf. speech by Anatole France, quoted in *le Progrès Civique*, February 25, 1922, where he states that Caillaux was condemned ' in accordance with orders received from the government ' and paid the penalty of having introduced the income-tax and kept Europe at peace in 1911.

The ' Ligue ' is a (theoretically) non-party organization founded in 1899 for the realization of the Republican spirit in France and the protection of individuals from the arbitrary action of the executive. But, like the new ' Ligue de la République ', founded by M. Painlevé, it is virtually an offshoot of the Radical party and is wedded to anti-clericalism and pacifism.

nationalist. The old majority section, formerly in favour of war credits, only received 337 votes out of 5,000, and most of its members withdrew from the party and formed the 'French Socialist Party', under the leadership of MM. Aubriot and Renard. The next step was the formal entry of the Socialist party into the Moscow International by a resolution passed at Tours in December 1920, but this led to a graver split than that of March. The elements unwilling to accept the conditions laid down by Moscow seceded and formed a new party which, although a minority in the congress, comprised the vast majority (57) of the 69 Socialist deputies in the Chamber. This party affiliated to the 'Vienna' International, formed by the union of those Socialist elements who could not accept Moscow conditions, but had no wish to return to the 'Second' International, in which the French Socialist party remained.[1] The unity of French Socialism, for which Jaurès sacrificed his cherished scheme of co-operation with the Radicals, is thus now a thing of the past. But this does not mean that there is an important number of Socialists prepared to co-operate with bourgeois parties on a constructive programme. The leader of the new party, Longuet, hostile to 'Moscow sectarianism', is not less anxious for the overthrow of the present system. French Socialism has largely abandoned the old idea that the revolution could come about by the Socialists obtaining a majority in Parliament and forming a Socialist ministry, and there is little left of the reformist Socialism, of which M. Millerand was once the apostle, which seeks to solve the social problem by gradually bringing production under the control of the State. But although the virtual adoption by Socialists of Syndicalist theories means that the party is bound to be in formal opposition to every bourgeois cabinet, Radical as well as Conservative, Socialist votes can be depended upon for particular measures of an anti-militarist or anti-capitalist character ; and there are indications that in its present disorganization and weak-

[1] See in the *Nation*, January 7, 1922, an illuminating letter by Longuet showing the present international distribution of the various Socialist parties in Europe.

ness, the Socialist party would not be averse to some temporary working agreement with other parties of the Left on the basis of industrial nationalization, proportional representation, and disarmament.[1]

Syndicalism, as we said, was pursuing meanwhile a different evolution. During the war the C.G.T. remained prepared to help the Government, though it demanded the repression of the censorship, denounced intervention against the Soviets, and attacked the peace of Versailles. The war over, it put forward a series of ' minimum demands ', which (apart from some purely economic items) comprised an 8-hour day in all industries, the reconstruction of the devastated regions by collective organization of producers, consumers, and officials, and the appropriation by the State of anything approaching a monopoly, which should be transferred to the control of decentralized and autonomous groupings of producers, consumers, and officials. Of these demands only the first, the universal 8-hour day and 48-hour week, was granted by a law passed in April 1919. The enormous increase in the cost of living during the next few months and the virtual refusal of many organizations to apply the 8-hour law led to deep restlessness, which culminated in a series of strikes ; first a railway strike in February 1920, then a miners' strike in March, and finally an attempt at a general strike in May. The strike was a complete failure. There was not sufficient agreement among the various unions, and the only result was a great weakening of the C.G.T. A number of syndicates withdrew bodily, and it is estimated that the total membership was reduced by a half.[2] These defections came equally from the Bolshevist elements, who reproached the C.G.T. for the mildness of its programme, and from the Moderates, who disapproved of a general strike for virtually political ends.

[1] See the Minutes of the Congress held in Paris in October 1921. ' Without concluding any treaty of alliance they hold out an open hand to any parties of the Left that will help them to realize this programme ' (*Progrès Civique*, November 5, 1921).

For other indications of this tendency towards Radical and Socialist co-operation, see articles in the *Temps*, March 12, 13, and 16, 1922.

[2] From 1,350,000 to 600,000, said M. Faure, at the Socialist Congress of June, 1920 (quoted in *la Revue de Paris*, March 15, 1921).

The failure of the strike, therefore, left the internal situation of the C.G.T. much as it was before ; it only accentuated an already existing cleavage between those who saw in Russia the logical application of Syndicalist principles and those whom events in Russia led to a reconsidering and modifying of their tenets. But whereas among the Socialists this same conflict culminated in a victory for Moscow, in the C.G.T. the Moderates prevailed. At a congress held at Orleans in October 1920, it was decided to keep the C.G.T. absolutely free from union with any political organization, and not to affiliate to the Third International. This does not mean that French Syndicalism has given up its political programme, or its international and anti-militarist principles ; but that its leaders have for the moment dropped revolutionary tactics and that the C.G.T. keeps its entire freedom of action on any issue that may arise.

It should be added that, strictly speaking, the C.G.T. is no longer a legal body. The government took strong steps to make any future attempts at a general strike futile : not only were 25,000 railway men dismissed, but the C.G.T. itself was dissolved by a ministerial decree. This measure was merely a dramatic gesture to reassure the frightened bourgeoisie : no government could, as a matter of fact, dissolve an organization of that character, however weakened and divided ; and the decree was simply ignored. But that the government should have taken the step shows to what extent the C.G.T. has lost the powers it once wielded. The phenomenon need not surprise us : one of the results of the war seems to have been that organized labour has everywhere either seized the reins of government in its own hands, or lost much of the ground it had won in earlier years. The main point at issue in France seems to be at present whether the trade unions will be able to resist the pressure which the employers are putting on the government for the repeal of the 8-hours' day.[1] However divided and weakened, both Syndicalism and Socialism are still forces to be reckoned

[1] The General Syndicate of Commerce and Industry, a federation of employers, has just passed a strongly worded resolution in that direction (*Temps*, March 12, 1922).

with. We saw that the apparent setback given to the latter at the 1919 elections was illusory, the total Socialist poll having increased from 1914 ; and Socialists of various shades still form probably the largest homogeneous fraction of the electorate (nearly one quarter of the whole).

§ 4. *Classes and Parties*

Before we can answer the question of the probable development of Socialism, we must first ask to what extent are party divisions identical with class divisions. A very rough classification might identify Royalism with what remains of the old aristocracy, Conservative republicanism with the wealthy bourgeoisie, Radicalism with the middle and lower middle class, and Socialism with the industrial urban population.[1] But exceptions to this rule are so numerous that it really helps us very little. The lower middle class or ' petite bourgeoisie ' contains some of the most conservative elements in the country, namely small investors in State funds ; the Socialist party has members in almost every class of society ; and the wealthy bourgeoisie continues to supply leaders to all political parties and organizations, from the Action Française to the Communist ' Clarté '.

The classification referred to has also the grave disadvantage of ignoring two important elements of the French social organism, the Professions and the Peasantry. The former are almost a class by themselves in so far as cheap education makes the professional class accessible to many a man born in a lower rank of life—barristers, doctors, journalists, and especially school masters are to be found in all parties, and the French respect for things of the mind enables members of those professions to exert in politics an influence greatly in excess of their mere numbers. As to the peasants, far from being attached to one party or another, they tend to be indifferent to politics and only become interested if any measure is proposed which threatens one of their privileges—from

[1] The growth of Socialism corresponds very exactly with the exodus from the country to the town and with the large increase in urban population.

private property in land to the right of vine-growers to distil their own alcohol. On the whole the peasant vote tends to be conservative in the non-political sense of the term ; the sitting member for an agricultural constituency is not likely to be disturbed unless he is accused of having unduly neglected the interests of his constituents, and the distribution of parties in rural France has scarcely changed since 1848, certain areas such as Brittany being steadfastly Conservative, while the south-east has strong Radical traditions.

While therefore there are many among the bourgeoisie who are not averse to drastic changes in the political and economic framework of the country, any movement towards a social revolution is certain to encounter the opposition of two classes, the ' rentiers ' and the peasantry, who, while vanquishable separately, would form together a formidable barrier. The proletariat can only establish its dictatorship either by guaranteeing to pay the interest on State bonds, so as to conciliate the petite bourgeoisie, or by securing the co-operation of the peasantry : and this can only be done by abandoning one of its most fundamental principles and allowing the continuation of private property in land. At the 1919 elections the Socialist party made an attempt to capture the peasant vote. It issued a manifesto declaring that ' Socialism is not solely concerned with the interests of industrial workers ; that it wishes to bring back to the rural workers themselves the means of production, and does not struggle against the small owners who themselves produce.' But the appeal failed. It is difficult for the peasant mind to differentiate between Syndicalists and Socialists, between the Socialist party and the mass of town industrial workers ; and one of the results of the war has been to make the French peasants deeply hostile to the urban population. They allege that they bore the brunt of the war while the factory hand was ' embusqué ' in certified trades. The townsman replies that the war mainly destroyed the industrial north and hardly touched the French agricultural countryside ; that the war crippled the trades unions and enriched the peasant. That all these accusations are partisan and highly coloured is obvious ; we need only point out how unlikely it is that these two classes will soon co-operate in order to overthrow the present system. France in fact is an illustration of Dr. Haden Guest's contention [1] that party conflicts are gradually discarding old divisions and becoming an adjustment of claims between town and agricultural workers—the clash between the ' Red ' communism of the towns and the ' Green ' communism of the countryside as expressed in the manifesto of the Bulgarian Peasant Party. In no country is that conflict likely to be more acute than in France.

CONCLUSION

It is now possible to sum up the general results of this study. Our analysis has shown that three main issues lie at the foundation of French party divisions and still dominate French politics.

The first is the religious problem, caused by the difficulty of reconciling the Republican and Catholic ideals of society in a country where the Church had once enjoyed an unquestioned supremacy both as a spiritual and as a temporal power. Neither side has so far evinced any desire to find a basis of co-operation, and Cavour's formula of ' the free church in the free state ' seems as far as ever from being realized, so long as each tries to realize its freedom by limiting the freedom of the other. Yet without some religious settlement, based on a spirit of toleration in which clericals and anti-clericals alike seem to be entirely lacking, there can be little hope of internal peace or cohesion.

The second is the problem of industrial organization and the policy to be adopted by governments towards parties and organizations of a frankly revolutionary character. Are Syndicalism and Communism on the one hand, and Monarchism on the other, philosophies so dangerous as to need repressing by the same methods as were once used for the suppression of republican propaganda ? Is it wrong to employ communist teachers in

[1] *The Struggle for Power in Europe*, p. 253.

elementary schools,[1] or to entrust to a non-Republican
Catholic the teaching of political philosophy ? Should
the army be used for strike breaking ? Should the
syndicates of civil servants be dissolved ? [2] And this
raises the further question of the relation of the State
to any organization—political club, trade guild, or Church
—whose growing power may become a real danger to the
sovereignty of the State itself ; a problem that involves
the most fundamental issues in political philosophy and
demands for its solution the highest statesmanship.[3]

The third is the problem of foreign affairs, or more
exactly of Franco-German relations. Can France and
Germany find some basis, if not of complete reconciliation,
at least of co-operation towards the restoration of a
common international life, or are they destined to remain
for ever mutually hostile and distrustful ? Is the League
of Nations an adequate guarantee of national security ?
Here again a new attitude of mind is wanted, of which
few signs are as yet visible on either side ; but on the
settlement of this feud depends the future peace of
Europe.

All these are pre-war problems, and the only effects
of the war on politics have been to increase the urgency
of international and industrial questions and to alter
the balance of power between the parties. When every
allowance has been made for the unsatisfactory character
of the system of voting, the voice of France in 1919 was

[1] In June 1921 and January 1922 the Minister of Education sent out
circulars ordering the prosecution of teachers who subscribed to communist papers, or ' who held opinions subversive of the French
Republican State '. A woman teacher was recently dismissed for
having signed a communist manifesto. As far back as 1905, M. Dubief,
then Minister of the Interior, declared that ' the government would not
surrender the right to know the attitude of its servants towards the
Republic ' (Laski, op. cit., p. 330).

[2] ' French Civil Servants' Unions abolished.—A French Government
order issued some time ago prohibited the formation or maintenance of
trades unions of Government employees, such as postal employees,
teachers in State schools, Custom employees, &c. These organizations,
however, ignored the official ruling, and continued in existence. Eleven
trades unions of civil servants have now been dissolved by the Criminal
Court, the representatives of the Unions being also fined 100 francs.—
Reuter.' Yorkshire Post, March 14, 1922.

[3] See Laski, op. cit., and the works of Professors Duguit and Esmein.

emphatic : it dismissed the Radicals from office and recalled the Conservatives ; and even if there has been since some movement from the Right to the Left, it is certain that a cabinet like M. Poincaré's is not unrepresentative of public opinion.[1]

Whichever party is in power, the violence of party conflict has certainly not abated as a result of the war. The cause of this violence has already been noticed : it lies in the fact that the fundamentals of social, political, and religious organization are all in dispute, and that there has rarely been a middle party able to prevent either extreme from pursuing its policy in flagrant disregard of anybody else's interests. Each party sees in its tenure of power an opportunity for revenge for previous persecution. The minority cannot trust the majority for fair treatment, and the result is that the ultimate recourse to force is rarely entirely absent from the mind of politicians : there is what Lord Bryce calls a legacy of revolutionary habits. ' Direct Action ' is not the monopoly of Syndicalists or Communists ; it is preached with equal vigour on the extreme Right ; and it is an almost unavoidable weapon against the arbitrary and often illegal exercise by the executive of its enormous powers.

We see therefore no reason to believe that France is entering upon a period in which party conflicts will be laid aside in order that all should unite on ' national issues '. Such phraseology assumes that all parties and people really have the same view of what constitutes national welfare, but it is curious to note how invariably this supposed unanimity coincides with the speaker's particular view. The fact is that there are now, and there always have been, widely diverging views of what is, or should be, the ' real France '. Is it that of Pascal or of Voltaire, of Rousseau or of Napoleon, of Jaurès or of Barrès ? Was the French Revolution a disaster or

---

[1] It is typical of the present conservatism of French politics that of the two anniversaries of 1921, the centenary of Napoleon's death in May was officially celebrated with much more pomp and circumstance than the jubilee of the Republic in September. *Vide* the French press for those two months, *passim*.

a blessing? Between those rival philosophies it seems impossible to establish a common basis of agreement.[1]

It seems to us on the contrary that in no country has any real national unity proved more impossible of attainment. We have already commented upon the extreme individualism which wrecks party discipline and organization and leads to sterility of political and social achievement. This individualism we would ascribe to two factors in the national temperament—an intellectual keenness that produces strongly-held beliefs and creates political and religious (or anti-religious) fanatics : and an anarchical tendency which leads to resentment of authority, to reluctance to work as one of a team and to sink one's personality into an anonymous unit.

It is not therefore by a centralized uniformity which can only be imposed and maintained by coercion that France will best fit herself for her task in the world of to-morrow, but by her recognition in her institutions of the extraordinary richness and variety of her national life and genius.

[1] See on this question, Seippel, *Les deux Frances* (1912). In his preface to Gaston Riou's *Aux écoutes de la France qui vient* (1913), M. Faguet sketches a 'third France, neither the France of Rome nor that of Geneva, less noisy than either, but much greater ' ; but his contention that this is ' the real France, France herself ' only illustrates, in our judgement, the impossibility of such identifications. See also V. Giraud, *La troisième France* (1917), Guy-Grand and Dell, op. cit.

SUPPLEMENTARY CHAPTER 1922–1930

§ 1. *France and Europe*

THE history of Franco-German relations since 1922 is so integral a part of European affairs that the briefest of treatments will suffice. The years 1922 to 1924 witnessed the complete failure both of the ' strong hand ' method adopted by M. Poincaré and the parties of the Right to coerce Germany into the payment of reparations, and of all attempts at breaking up German unity by detaching from the Reich portions of the Rhineland alleged to be of ' separatist ' tendencies. The occupation by the French of the Ruhr district (Jan. 1923–Sept. 1924) only remains as a tragic example of the wrong way of carrying on international relations. Fortunately Radicals and Socialists realized in time the folly of the policy, and together fought the elections of 1924 on the issue of a peaceful settlement with Germany. The victory of the ' Cartel of the Left ', as this electoral alliance was called, placed Franco-German relations on a new footing, and the policy of Herriot and Briand, to whose name should be added that of Stresemann, led successively to the settlement of Reparations by the Dawes and Young Plans, to the mutual guarantee of existing frontiers under British sanction by the Locarno agreements, to the entrance of Germany into the League of Nations, and to the evacuation of the whole Rhineland at a date considerably earlier than that anticipated in the treaty of Versailles. Not only did this policy represent a great achievement of constructive statesmanship, but it led to a breaking down of most of the psychological barriers, which had for so many years divided French and Germans ; except for a handful of irreconcilables on both sides, the two peoples seem to be entering into an era, if not of close friendship as yet, at least of close political and economic co-operation.

If a steady improvement has marked the relations of France with Germany, the same unfortunately cannot be said of her relations with her other chief continental neighbour, Italy. A certain tenseness in Franco-Italian relations soon followed upon the establishment of Fascism, some of the wilder elements of that party making statements about the return to the Italian Motherland of Nice, Savoy, and Corsica which could not but arouse apprehension in French minds. One of the effects of this new phase of ' Irredentism ' was the early severance of those psychological links which originally bound together Italian Fascists and the French ' Caesarist ' groups : the nationalism of the latter made them see in the former potential enemies rather than colleagues pursuing an identical policy in their respective countries.

Of Franco-British relations during the period little need be said. The friendship between the two countries has undergone some fluctuations, and considerable divergences of opinion appeared at times, particularly when M. Poincaré and Lord Curzon ruled over their respective Foreign Offices, and on a later occasion, when British public opinion feared that a separate naval agreement with France might jeopardize our good relations with the United States. The desire to remain friends has, however, invariably triumphed so far over possible misunderstandings and quarrels. Towards the East of Europe, France's close co-operation with the ' Petite Entente ' has remained unbroken, and diplomatic relations with Russia, resumed in 1924, have been maintained since without interruption.

§ 2. *The Financial Problem*

The failure of the Cartel in domestic was not less marked than its success in foreign affairs. After a successful expulsion of M. Millerand from the Presidency of the Republic, Finance Ministers followed one another in quick succession in vain attempts to balance the budget and to prevent the depreciation of the currency which had steadily been going on since 1919, until in July 1926, with the franc standing at 250 to the pound, it became clear that the cabinet-forming power of the Left Wing Parties had become exhausted : M. Poincaré then succeeded both in forming a ' National Union ' cabinet, including the Radical leaders Herriot and Painlevé and the internationalist Briand, and in saving the financial situation, ultimately stabilizing the currency at 124·5 francs to the pound.

This return to power of the very man for whose over-throw the existing Parliament had been apparently elected can be fairly easily explained. The election of 1924 had been fought almost entirely for or against Poincarist foreign policy ; but two years of Cartellism had given Western Europe a real chance of permanent peace, and there was no danger now of a reversal. On the other hand, the Cartel had no unity in its financial policy. Its Socialist and advanced Radical elements wanted to solve the problem by ' taking money where it was to be found '— i.e. by the heavy taxation of the rich, either by a capital levy or by a great stiffening of the income tax. The more moderate Cartellists were afraid of such drastic steps as would frighten the wealthy bourgeoisie, and inclined to the more conservative solutions of higher indirect taxation, cutting down of state expenses, and generally to a policy of ' reassuring ' capital and inducing it to remain invested in national undertakings instead of being sent abroad, in defiance of the existing legislation forbidding its expor-tation. There was therefore from the very beginning a division of counsels, which made a clear policy and there-fore a stable government impossible as soon as the centre of affairs shifted from foreign to financial policy. In this respect the return to politics of M. Caillaux was paradoxi-cal beyond measure. Pardoned by the Amnesty Bill of 1924 and soon elected to the Senate, he was brought into the Cabinet by M. Painlevé in April 1925 without any serious protests being raised, but resigned in October owing to the Radical insistence on a Capital levy which, as a ' Bourgeois ' financier, he could not accept ; his later return to office with M. Briand in June 1926 was hailed by the Conservatives as a victory for ' sound ' finance, his fall on July 17 being due to Radical opposition to the semi-dictatorial powers he demanded as the essential condition to financial reconstruction.

Mere disunion was not the only cause for the Cartellist failure in finance. The incompetence of its Finance Ministers has often been urged, but it may fairly be asked whether these really had a fair chance. Their real diffi-culty was the lack of that elusive thing called ' confidence ' which plays so large a part in the maintenance of national credit. Distrust in a party combination that was in constant need of socialist support was widespread and not unnatural in certain quarters, but the allegation cannot be altogether denied that powerful interests were at work who were determined that, come what may to the franc, the parties of the Left should not be allowed to construct a financial settlement on a basis implying a complete break with the existing traditions of French finance. The comparative ease with which M. Poincaré ' stopped the rot' in a few weeks seems to indicate that others could have triumphed if they had been given the moral and material support which his personality was able to command.

§ 3.   *Party Struggles*

The solid majority of nearly all parties, excluding Socialists and Communists, which M. Poincaré had been able to maintain as long as the financial problem remained unsettled remained outwardly unbroken for well over two years. It is true that the extreme Right disliked his complete abdication of foreign policy into the hands of Briand, while the Radicals naturally chafed at being under the leadership of their former enemy—but the dread of return to the financial chaos of 1925-6 prevented any outward denunciation of the party truce which had saved the franc, and it was still as the head of a ' national union ' ministry that M. Poincaré faced the General Election of 1928. The verdict was a clear vote of confidence, the majority of the successful candidates affirming their belief in him as the only possible Prime Minister, while making it clear that this allegiance was personal and would not be necessarily transferred to his eventual successor. But even then this support came from the Centre and Right rather than from the Left ; the Radical support was wearing very thin, the mass of the party feeling increasingly as they had in 1924 that their natural political allies were more in the Socialist than in the Conservative ranks.

The break came in November 1928, with the temporary re-emergence of the old anticlerical issue. The pressure of financial and foreign problems had prevented the Cartel from renewing the war against the Church—two attempts had indeed been made, one to suppress the French embassy at the Vatican, the other to introduce the ' lay laws ' into Alsace (see below), but both had failed, and the only success of the Left Parties had been the negative one of preventing any relaxation of existing legislation against Catholic orders. But in the Budget for 1929 two clauses appeared, of little importance in themselves, but which appeared to Radicals and Socialists alike as violating the canons of anti-clerical orthodoxy; as a result of this the Radical congress assembled at Angers demanded the resignation of Radical Ministers from the Cabinet. The Cabinet was re-formed, minus the Radicals and minus also its most conservative member, M. Marin, jettisoned to keep some kind of party balance. In July 1929 M. Poincaré handed over the premiership to M. Briand : health partly, but also reluctance to be responsible for the Reparations agreements about to be signed at The Hague. In November Briand was defeated by a combination of Right and Left, the latter voting against the Hague policy of which they approved in order to overthrow the government. Having headed the opposition, M. Daladier, who had succeeded M. Herriot as leader of the Radicals, was asked to form a ministry, but the Socialist party refused, by a small majority, to share with the Radicals the responsibility of office, thus remaining faithful to the old ' anti-partici-pationist ' tradition. M. Daladier then vainly tried to unite Radical and Centre parties : after a government-less fortnight of discussion [1] M. Tardieu, minister of the Interior in the last two Cabinets, and for some years the ' coming man ' of the anti-Socialist Centre groups, was called to office and successfully continued the coalition of Central and moderate Conservative groups formed by M. Poincaré after the Radicals' withdrawal. Defeated last February on a minor issue, he returned to power after the three days' fiasco of a Radical-Centre coalition under M. Chautemps. The peculiar feature of these crises was the part played therein by the congresses of the Radical and Socialist parties on whose decisions hung the fate of Cabinets. This ' interference ' of party organizations ' unknown to

[1] On which see Privat, *Les heures d'André Tardieu et la crise des partis.*

the constitution', strongly resented as it was by those not of the Left, taken together with the undoubted stiffening of party discipline among the groups of the Right, marks a distinct advance on the party chaos which has so far been the bane of French politics. The ' Union Républicaine Démocratique', led by M. Marin, is fast becoming a well organized party, round which are rallying all those who share its rooted opposition to the economic and international programmes of Socialism. It remains to be seen whether the disruptive tendencies of the French group system will wreck once more this attempt at forming the Conservative counterpart of the Radical, Socialist, and Communist parties. These four organizations, or five, if we add the weakening remnants of Royalist supporters, would represent accurately enough the four main currents of political opinion, remembering always the existence, between the Marin and Herriot tendencies, of border-line groups who support Radical anticlericalism while distrusting co-operation with the Socialists.

§ 4.   *Church and State*

Of problems not directly contributing to the making and unmaking of Cabinets, two deserve special mention, both of them closely connected with religious affairs, Alsatian autonomism and the condemnation of the ' Action Française '. The reunion of Alsace to France found the rigid administrative system of France in no wise prepared for the reassimilation into an irreligious centralized State of a German-speaking territory which, during its fifty years of separation, had developed strong local institutions and, in the name of Alsatian Nationalism, had tightened ecclesiastical control, Catholic, Protestant, and Jewish, over its elementary schools. The kaleidoscopic changes in the French policy during the years immediately following the peace, from one of liberal home rule to harsh unification, the exasperating slowness of an inefficient administration which did not even understand the language of the people, the attempt to treat the native tongue as a foreign language, the levying of the ordinary French taxation in addition to the already heavy system of local taxation—all this rapidly destroyed the joy of reunion and created deep-seated unrest, which manifested itself in the formation of an avowedly autonomist party. Separation from France and return to Germany was not suggested, and indeed some of the leaders had been prominent in the defence of Alsatian liberties in the days of German occupation ; but the right for Alsace to live her own life as a federated not an assimilated section of France was affirmed, in blank negation to the unitary principle on which the French political structure had been built. The half-hearted attempts at religious unification made by the Herriot Cabinet in 1924 (threats to place the schools under entire State control and to break the Concordat under which the Church in Alsace is still established) had to be hastily withdrawn owing to the storm it raised among all, even non-autonomist, circles ; but autonomism went on growing, until in 1926 the Poincaré Cabinet attempted a policy of open repression, suppressing its papers and finally arresting its leader on a charge of treason. The 1928 election, held while the Home Rulers were still awaiting trial, led to the triumphant election of a number of auto-nomists including two of the prisoners ; and the Colmar trial, which resulted in the condemnation of four out of fifteen accused by a bare majority of seven to five, caused serious rioting and bade fair to break what remained of loyalty to France in the great mass of Alsatian opinion. The Government fortunately realized it had gone too far, and a few months later an amnesty bill marked its retreat from an untenable position. Autonomist propaganda may now be said to be tolerated ; and the next generation will probably be less reluctant to fit into the French system—provided always the privileges of the Churches are left unchallenged. But such a lack of uniformity in religious policy is so contrary to all French political traditions that it is difficult to see how long such a dualism can endure ; autonomism has certainly acted as a rude challenge to the French dogmas of uniform centralization, and put the problem of regional Home Rule into the very forefront of domestic politics.

The condemnation of the ' Action Française ' by the Papacy, which has been described as ' the most severe disciplinary action of the Holy See in modern times ', goes of course far beyond the limits of mere ecclesiastical policy. As a result of a series of measures taken in 1926,[1] membership of the movement and the reading of the newspaper *L'Action Française* were forbidden to all Catholics, any who rebelled being denied the sacraments and religious marriage. It was indeed a complete severance of the Church from a movement which had hitherto boasted of standing for Catholic interests and of receiving quasi-official Catholic support.

Various reasons, many of them absurd,[2] have been given for so unprecedented a step, the true explanation being that the times seemed ripe for a return to Leo XIII's *Ralliement* policy of 1893. Anticlericalism was no longer a live issue ; a *modus vivendi* had been arranged by which Diocesan associations, accepted both by Papacy and Government, took over legal administration of Church affairs ; the Poincaré Government had been anxious to meet the Church more than half way over the Alsatian question, and if the full reconciliation of Vatican and Republic, which alone the complete abrogation of all anticlerical legislation could achieve, was not yet realizable, a long and healing truce could certainly be envisaged—the only obstacle to which was the persistent and savage onslaught waged upon the whole Republican system by the extreme Catholic conservatism of which the ' Action Française ' was the spokesman. No religious truce was thus possible without the disassociation of the Catholic cause from that noisy and unscrupulous body, the ardent bellicosity of which was also a hindrance to the Papal policy of international reconciliation.

§ 5. *The Present State of Parties*

The events of the last two years clearly show that if we exclude the two irreconcilable groups, Royalist Conservatives and Communists, the Chamber is divided into two approximately equal combinations. A majority to the Right appears whenever a crucial vote of fundamental policy is taken, and has so far prevented the formation of

---

[1] The actual decisions had been taken by the preceding Pope in 1914, and suspended because of war conditions.

[2] See Gwynn, *The Condemnation of the Action Française.*

any Cabinet acceptable to the Socialists; but many decisions of some importance have been taken favourable to the Left, as for instance the gradual introduction of gratuity into secondary schools, the unification of the elementary system with the lower forms of the secondary schools, and the passing of the law on Social Insurance, in spite of violent protests from the Right—not forgetting, of course, the carrying on of the Briand tradition in foreign affairs.

On the whole, we may note the weakening both of the extreme Right and of anticlerical Radicalism, together with the strengthening of the Centre groups and of the Socialist and Communist parties. The last two lost seats in 1928, but their total poll increased considerably. Far from being a diminishing force, Communism is an ever-increasing challenge to the established rule, and the violence of the anti-Communist campaign, of which M. Tardieu has been the leader since he became minister of the Interior, shows the fear in which it is held by the bourgeois parties. There is, on the other hand, no indication that a Socialist Cabinet, even in a minority, is likely to be in office during the present Parliament; what the elections of 1932 will bring forth no one can tell at present.

If we pass on from party divisions to present issues, it would appear that the religious problem is now at least dormant, and that on both sides there is a genuine desire to maintain those compromises which prevent violent strife. Any attempt, however, either on the part of anti-clericalism to force its solution on the Alsatian Churches or on the part of the Church to secure the removal of present restrictions would infallibly rekindle fires that can never be wholly extinguished. The second problem, that of Franco-German relations, is happily virtually solved; a reversal of M. Briand's policy seems altogether outside practical politics. How much further France is prepared to go, particularly as regards disarmament, appears doubtful: her faith in international agreement as guaranteeing security is obviously very small as yet.

There remains the third problem, which is further than ever from any solution, the attitude of the State towards corporate bodies, whether professional or geographical.

Alsatian autonomism, administrative syndicalism, militant trade-unionism are three aspects of the same problem, the contemporary challenge to the sovereign state.

Fourthly and lastly there remains the Communist threat to the existing social and economic order. The acute quarrel now raging between Socialists and Communists, each struggling for the mastery of the working-class world, is of course a valuable asset to the bourgeois parties ; but such controversy seems inevitable as long as Communism remains directly controlled by Moscow, while Socialism is divided between the vague reformism of a Paul Boncour and the quasi-Marxism of a Léon Blum.

There are on the whole no indications of any startling changes in the distribution of political power or in the general tendencies of French political life. In spite of some intensification of feminist propaganda, Women's Suffrage appears to be as far off as ever : it has many individual supporters, but no party is prepared as yet to place it upon its programme. The anti-Parliamentarian ' Caesarist ' forces have been seriously weakened, both by the condemnation of the ' Action française ' and by the anti-French attitude of Italian Fascism, and it is probably true to say that in the essential features of her political and social organization, France remains one of the most fundamentally conservative of the countries of to-day.

BIBLIOGRAPHY

Fuller indications on special topics will be found in the notes. It is only proposed to mention here the chief books written in English to which reference should first be made for any further study.

History of the Third Republic :

Bodley. Article on France in the *Encyclopaedia Britannica*, eleventh edition. This stops at 1909, but is the fullest account for the years from 1896.

Bourgeois. *Modern France* (Cambridge Modern Historical Series, 1920).

—— Chapters in the *Cambridge Modern History* (to 1906).

Guérard. *French Civilization in the Nineteenth Century* (Fisher Unwin, 1914).

Seignobos. *Political Development of Contemporary Europe* (Heinemann, 1915). Invaluable for the period 1871 to 1895.

Politics and Parties :

Bodley. *France* (Macmillan, 1907). This work still forms an essential introduction to any serious study.

Bryce. *Modern Democracies* (Macmillan, 1921). Probably the most authoritative up-to-date study.

Buell. *Contemporary French Politics* (Appleton, 1920). Although lacking the touch of personal knowledge, this book contains much valuable information.

Dell. *My Second Country, France* (John Lane, 1920). An illuminating survey, based on an intimate acquaintance with French life : invaluable in spite of its marked Socialist bias.

Dimnet (Abbé). *France Herself Again* (Chatto & Windus, 1914). Very conservative.

George. *France in the Twentieth Century* (Alston Rivers, 1908). Anti-clerical.

Huddleston, *France* (Benn, 1926).

Siegfried, *France, a Study in Nationality* (Oxford Press, 1930).

Soltau, *French Political Thought in the Nineteenth Century* (Benn, 1930).

Institutions :

Finer. *Foreign Governments at Work* (World of To-day Series, 1922).

Lovell. *Governments and Parties in Continental Europe* (Longmans, 1918).

Poincaré. *How France is Governed* (Fisher Unwin, 1913).

Sait. *Government and Politics of France* (Harrap, 1920).

INDEX

This index has been limited to proper names occurring more than once, and to such topics as cannot be immediately identified by reference to the table of contents.

Date Due

Demco 38-297